Daryl A. Bell

May

D0900110

Personalities of the Old Testament

Personalities
of the
Old Testament

by
Ralph G. Turnbull

BAKER BOOK HOUSE

Grand Rapids, Michigan
1964

Library of Congress Catalog Card Number: 64-15681

PHOTOLITHOPRINTED BY CUSHING - MALLOY, INC.
ANN ARBOR, MICHIGAN, UNITED STATES OF AMERICA
1964

Dedicated

to

Granville C. Henry,

John H. Woodson,

sons-in-law;

Jonnie D. Turnbull,

Sharon B. Turnbull,

daughters-in-law

Introduction

This volume is a companion to *Personalities of the New Testament* issued in 1960. There I referred to the romance behind the writings as seen through fascinating personalities. The Old Testament also is full of dramatic incident and is like a portrait gallery of people who are depicted on canvas in unfading colors.

The rich and colorful human element makes a perennial appeal. We feel the pulse and thrill in every phase of activity. Here are no puppets for mechanical manipulation but "flesh and blood," "warts and all," of people like ourselves. Trial and temptation, sinning and overcoming, are there but always under divine providence.

William Shakespeare's characters are drawn out of every age in their mixture of good and evil. The Old Testament is not behind in its literary craftsmanship in giving us these samples of human nature. Like a mirror we see ourselves in these lives. By understanding and sympathy we "sit where they sit." I only hope that a preacher's treatment with certain images and ideas will not dull the original canvas.

Ralph G. Turnbull

The First Presbyterian Church
of Seattle, Washington
January, 1964

Contents

Miriam,
A Leader in Israel

One of the surprises in Bible study is to find the place given to women. We expect this in the New Testament because of the place given by our Lord Jesus Christ. He gathered many as disciples to follow him. He received the ministration of some when he went about doing good and needed hospitality for himself and his friends. His message transformed the thinking of the ancient world by giving a new status to women and a place in the Christian church. The Old Testament has accepted their place as more subordinate in the light of the customs and socially accepted procedures of family life. Then a woman rarely found an opportunity to do anything outside the home. In this light we find the story of Miriam assuming a significance which is outstanding and rare. There are others in the Old Testament record who find a niche in the making of history and Miriam is one of the first. The references are few and point to the incidental yet vital part she played in relation to her brothers as they led the Israelites out of bondage into freedom.

I. The Sister of Moses and Aaron

This in itself was a distinction for anyone! To be born into this particular family gave her a social position far above the other women of Israel. She belonged to the leading family. Her parents may not have been so designated (cf. I Chron. 6:3)—"the children of Amram" whose family background is not too important in the divine story as so recorded. Gifts and ability were inherited from those who went before her and her heritage was one of strength and hope. Amram is listed as a son of Kohath, the son of Levi (cf. Exod. 6:18; Num. 3:19), and as a descendent of that group was privileged in position and service. The influence upon Miriam lay in the direction of priestly service and ministration in connection with the worship of God. Like her brothers she shared in that godly heritage.

The realism of her position is seen in that she always played a subordinate place to her brothers, especially Moses. She was the eldest and from the beginning she had watched over them. It began with the birth of Moses and how she saved his life by the clever unfolding of the actions by the water and the bulrushes when the princess of Egypt came to bathe. The cry of the child led to the intervention of Miriam with her suggestion to secure a nurse (Exod. 2:1-10). She stood by watching and waiting for this one moment to be grasped once and for all. Even as a young mother looking upon a new-born babe, she had mental quickness and physical dexterity to act in a decisive hour. Having saved her brother Moses from death in infancy it was not unreasonable to imagine that she always felt close to him and assumed that she could share his life and counsel. Perhaps she was about fifteen years of age or old enough to be at the dawn of womanhood with its attendant responsibilities. Shrewd and practical she knew how to take command of a delicate situation and in God's providence be a link in the saving of her nation.

As the sister of two illustrous men she had to take the second place. This was decreed by custom and inheritance. The woman's place in Israel was made much better and higher than that which was common to other nations around. She was no longer a mere chattel of man and certainly rose steadily in esteem and worth as the divine law became known and family life assumed greater sacredness. The man always led the family and Miriam's place could never be first. A single and unmarried woman was a rarity and an exception. How could she share in leadership except under very rare circumstances? The impression is given that she was a woman of strong character and of quick action. She had gifts of leadership and knew how to speak and to sing. As Moses was the *prophet* and Aaron the *priest* we may well think of Miriam as the *poet*. She had gifts of expression and stood closer to the people than the more exalted brothers whose offices separated them from the crowd. It has taken the civilized world a long time to afford women a place in the leadership of nations or positions in public life and the professions as well as in business. The home must ever abide as the supreme place where a woman's glory and mission are attained. However, in the providence of God there will always be the exceptional woman who finds outlet for gifts and ability in other walks of life. Miriam is the forerunner of all single—unmarried women who so find life.

II. Her Character Strong in Leadership

Exodus 15 records how Miriam displayed the characteristics of a leader. Moses was the divinely appointed leader of the nation, but Aaron his brother and now Miriam his sister shared in part of that. Later we shall see how this time of sharing led these two into trouble and danger. Incentive is to be encouraged but when it becomes interference then insult follows. The time was at the deliverance from Egypt and in the mighty deed of the Exodus. Slavery was behind these people and in the flush of this hard-won victory Miriam shared. She could not contain herself. Expression of how she felt is contained in the outburst of song and demonstration in dance.

The dance indicated a special feature of the religious practices of that day. We read that "David danced before Jehovah with all his might; and David was girded with a linen ephod. So David and all the house of Israel brought up the ark of Jehovah with shouting, and with the sound of the trumpet" (II Sam. 6:14, 15). In Psalm 149:2, 3 is the exhortation to Israel to "rejoice in him that made him: Let the children of Zion be joyful in their King. Let them praise his name in the dance: let them sing praises unto him with timbrel and harp." When David returned from the slaughter of the Philistines, "the women came out of all the cities of Israel, singing and dancing, to meet Saul. . ." (I Sam. 18:6). These choral exercises were obviously known and permitted as early as the Exodus. In this chapter of Exodus "Miriam took a timbrel and all the women went out after her with timbrels and with dances. And Miriam answered them, Sing ye to Jehovah, for he hath triumphed gloriously; The horse and the rider hath he thrown into the sea." The reference is to the whole *Song of Moses* recorded in this chapter.

The dance was not for social amusement but for a religious purpose. Allied to singing, its rhythmic movements expressed the joy and gratitude to God for his acts of deliverance. As Miriam led the singing she responded to the rest of the people in their outburst of thanksgiving. The song of deliverance told of praise to God because of the overthrow of the enemy. The victory was decisive. This means of commemoration gave scope to antiphonal choirs. Moses led his people and then Miriam gave answer. Miriam is spoken of as a prophetess (v. 20) and as such spoke. Her special gift was in song and thus the poetic strain is dominant in her speech. Here her leadership is exercised in strength and devotion. There is a fervency of utterance and a depth of feeling. God was highly exalted in this song. It was a "Magnificat" anticipating another to come in the New Testament by Mary the Mother of Jesus (cf. Luke 1:46-55). Miriam is seen here as one inspired and enthused as she led her women. At the sanctuary of Israel later, women played their part as well as men in religious exercises of song and dance. Miriam's song was the precursor of a tradition which has enriched sacred music in worship. If this is the first of the national anthems to swell the chorus of all nations, then Miriam is a noble exponent and example of impassioned song. How trite and feeble sounds our American National Anthem when crowds attempt to sing! It is likely that Miriam's leadership led a volume such as has scarcely been equalled in its power and audability!

III. Her Character Brittle with Jealousy

Leadership qualities are not to be despised. When God gives the endowment to a woman, men must acknowledge this and respond. When that leadership is based on character as well as ability, then strength is assured. Miriam gave evidence of this. As a prophetic leader she taught a nation to sing. The songs and hymns of a nation reflect

the spirit of a people. More than any eloquent address or
any dynamic sermon is the song that is hummed and sung
by generation after generation. As long as Miriam had her
place alongside of her brothers all was well. She increased
in her influence and power in Israel. But a change came
swiftly and tragically.

In Numbers 12 is the record of the change which came
over this woman. She defected from her high place of influence. She threw away in a moment her God-given
opportunity to share in the building of the nation. She
was no longer content to be "under Moses" as the leader
and share only in what was given her: she now usurped
that place by her actions and words. She now rebelled
against her brother and revealed a distorted vision of
what was right and proper "under God." A secret dis-
satisfaction creeps into her mind. She begins to compare
herself with her brother and the evil spirit of jealousy
smolders within. Several things led to this.

First, Moses had remarried. This time he took a
"foreigner" to wife, a woman from Cush or Ethiopia. The
wilderness journey had its subtle dangers of strain and
stress; its sameness and its monotony. Hitherto, Miriam
had shared most of Moses' life. With a new wife it was
natural that Miriam would no longer have the same intimate place in his life. Whether Moses was wrong in his
selection or not, the occasion revealed and drew out the
change in Miriam. One female jealous of another is an
easily recognized state of affairs. It intrudes into the
church as well as in all society. Miriam would be second
to Moses but not second to this woman! Her spleen and
jealousy resented this new personality as an intruder.
Loyalty to Moses is now tested and Miriam fails at this
point. Up to this time she had been prominent in the eyes

of the people, but now she would recede a little and she could not take that!

Secondly, the question of national leadership was involved. "Hath Jehovah indeed spoken only with Moses? hath he not spoken also by us?" (v. 2). Here is the crux of the situation. The social-family crisis was the occasion for this to break loose. Deep within Miriam was the thought that she was equal to Moses and could exercise leadership as he did. She was the instigator of the evil talk to her brother Aaron speaking against Moses. Her story is given in brief here but it is explosive in its reactions. She who guarded the ark of bulrushes for the child Moses and who led her women in song for victory now undoes the best years of her life! The spiritual and moral tragedy is unmasked in that one act and one word can spoil all the good things accomplished.

Fault-finding, evil-speaking, bickering, and a censoring judgment find expression. Although there was nothing wrong in Moses remarrying, to Miriam this was a mistake. She had decided not to play second fiddle any longer and certainly not to the new wife! She sensed that her brother Moses might not share as much with her as in former years. Her sister-in-law then became a rival and a hindrance to her own ambition. She saw the mote in her brother's eye but misses the beam in her own eye. The spirit of murmuring is an index of selfishness. The critic is born with a sneer and a bitter spirit. Such sin blights life and toil. It mars the sweetness and beauty of family relationships. It destroys the confidence and good-will among friends.

Miriam belittled Moses and his importance as God's supreme leader of Israel. She questioned his monopoly of divine revelation. She claimed equality with him. Because

Moses was truly "very meek" (v. 3), he paid no attention to this conniving against himself. He did not try to vindicate himself. God would do that and with decisive force! Jealousy burns like a fire (Ps. 79:5) and it is the rage of man (Prov. 6:34). It is also as cruel as the grave (Song of Songs 8:6). Love turns to hatred and trust is changed to suspicion. The torment of her mind found an outlet in defiling speech never to be retracted. Aaron does not seem to be the strong man at this point. He listens to his sister and she reveals herself in all her strength goaded on by jealousy and selfish ambition. Envy in the heart smolders a long time until it is fanned into a flame by some wind of desire and evil thought.

IV. Her Life Judged by God

In the midst of this conversation between Miriam and brother Aaron, God suddenly intervenes. Swift justice is done. Moses in contrast to his sister is seen as a man wronged and all the time aware of what is going on but never retaliating. God vindicates him swiftly and surely. God now speaks to the guilty pair and especially to Miriam. She is unmasked for what she is. God now tells them what he thinks of Moses and the high esteem in which he is held as the leader of Israel. We recall that Moses acknowledged when he was called of God that he was "slow of speech" (cf. Exod. 4:10). Was Miriam's sneer at him wedded to the idea in her mind that after all she had a facility of speech much freer and more compelling than his? (cf. Exod. 15:20). Because a person is not in the same class as another rarely leads to jealousy. It is the thrust of the mind which feels that somehow one is close to another or might become as the other if the chance is given that leads to this bane of jealousy. We might not compare ourselves with some of the great but we would write-down and write-off some on the same level as ourselves—and that with a sneer and an innuendo. Self-love is at the root of this evil spirit. We need not envy the gifts of others as Miriam, but rejoice in another's gifts if given by God and be content with our own for his service.

The back-biting is over now for God has spoken and the nemesis of her words has fallen upon her. Leprosy is her punishment. Smitten, she is rushed out of the camp to the solitude of the confinement reserved for those who are so stricken. God had spoken of Moses' "faithfulness" (v. 7) and thus reflected Miriam's unfaithfulness. She knew better God's ways and yet had sinned against light and knowledge. Now she takes the consequences. The disfigurement, the shame, the loneliness, the thought that all Israel knew of her defection and fall from high estate —all these things would be her companions of the sorrowful way of the leper. Worse still for the nation sharing in this was the fact that no progress was made for one week (v. 15). The pilgrimage was halted. God's judgment spoke of her as "one dead" and as one of whom they would be "ashamed" (vv. 12, 14). Aaron and Moses pleaded with God for her knowing full well her sin and shame. Meantime she was shut out from her people. She is listed as one "unclean," and therefore she is outside the fellowship of her people. She has no song or dance now, only slow steps which drag her feet and a heavy heart which has no lilt in it any more. All her so-called strength of character and her virile leadership have receded until she is a poor, weak, forsaken woman about to face death and the end.

V. The Mercy of the Lord

In Deuteronomy 24:9 it reads "Remember what the Lord did to Miriam, by the way as ye came forth out of Egypt." Nothing is worse than disobedience to the revealed will of God. Although Miriam's life ended in tragedy there is the suggestion of hope and recovery. She returned to the camp and the people marched forward again (Num. 12:15, 16). When Moses came to the end of his leadership on the borders of the Promised Land he addressed his people in farewell and valedictory. Among the many striking words was this word to them, "remember." One special stress was made that they should not forget Miriam. Her life and actions were to be held in memory for warning and yet inspiration. She had contributed much as a woman-leader of an emerging nation. She stood in the hour of transition from bondage to liberty with strength and resolution. She gave spirit and song to a new nation and inspired them to move forward. Looking back at her defection the summing up is clear and unmistakable—she had not only sinned, but it was "foolish" (Num. 12:11).

History must remember Miriam for her good qualities and be warned lest her tragedy be repeated. Other women leaders have made their contribution, not only in the nation but in the church. Catherine Booth of the Salvation Army and her daughter the Marechale (Mrs. Booth-Clibborn) of evangelistic gifts; Ida Scudder with her medical skill in India; the countless women missionaries throughout the world, and the unnumbered dedicated women who serve and give in the church militant. Miriam may well live on as an example of how a woman with gifts can find her place in the service of God.

God's mercy lay in his forgiving love which was asked

for on her behalf (Num. 12:11-14) and in judgment lay mercy. The afterward of regret, yet with healing, brought to Miriam the memories of other days—days when she watched over Moses, the man of God, as a child; days when she stood by her brothers in leadership of a nation. Her insight and persuasive words were useful then. Her epitaph lay in that men called her *the prophetess*. Near the Promised Land she died and never entered that destination—she had the "death in the desert" (Num. 20:1) with the echo of her song unforgotten.

2

Jethro,
A Practical Counselor

When the Exodus of Israel took place it is evident that others beside Israelites took the opportunity to escape. We read of "a mixed multitude" (Exod. 12:38). We have no word about Jethro, that he ever experienced the rigors of slavery. He appears on the stage of history in connection with Moses and the prophet's exile in the desert after he had fled from those who sought him for the killing of the Egyptians (Exod. 2:12). In the land of Midian, Moses and Jethro had met and the latter had given asylum to Moses. More than that—an alliance was entered into by marriage with Jethro's daughter. In this background we may discern much about the life and character of Jethro.

I. His Relationship to Moses, Exodus 4
Several things entered into this and should be seen in their relationship. First, Moses had fled from Egypt to escape the consequences of a crime. Some attempt may have been made to find him and bring him to justice but he escaped from the Egyptians. After wandering in the

desert he came to Jethro's people. Here he begins work
as a shepherd and for some forty years he is engaged in this
task. Long the days and the nights for an exile away from
his own kith and kin! Work is a therapeutic, and marriage
brings its compensations. It was natural that Moses would
marry into this family and find there an alliance of lasting
value. Jethro thus became Moses' father-in-law as well as
possibly his first employer!

Secondly, Moses finds that after the interval of the years
he must return to Egypt and help his people to escape
from slavery. That story is told in the book of Exodus
and its details are assumed in this context. After the
Exodus Moses brings his people to Mount Sinai and there
the Law and the Commandments are given by God. The
loosely linked slaves are now to begin the task of being
welded together as a nation "under God." Moses finds
this plagued with difficulty and trouble. There are many
set-backs linked with attacks from without and joined with
dissension within. After the foundation of nationhood is
laid Moses has the task of leadership all to himself. Aaron
and Miriam will share something of that work later, but
for a while Moses is alone. Jethro in his visit to his son-in-
law notices what is taking place and out of this gives his
counsel.

Another interesting item is mentioned about Jethro and
that is that he was "a priest of Midian" (Exod. 18:1). No
other word is given to interpret this. The Midianites were
a people of neighboring relationship. Descendants orig-
inally from Abraham, Midian was a son by his concubine
Keturah. His family line settled to the East of Caanan and
it was no accident that Moses fled there. There he also received his call to deliver Israel in Egypt. One of the
Midianites acted as guide "instead of eyes" in the wilder-

ness journey (Num. 10:29). Later, the Midianites were given to idolatry and ravaging wars and were further removed from Israel. However, at the time of Jethro there is no evidence that they were other than friendly to Israel. With their Abrahamic link Jethro seems to be a man with faith in God and a man with an open heart ready to bestow kindness and to be gracious to those in need. All this is not unrelated to his friendliness and acts of counsel to his son-in-law Moses. Who knows but that Jethro although not directly part of the Nation was at heart a man with the same spirit as Moses and with the same faith in the one true and living God?

II. His Knowledge of Human Need, Exodus 18

The spirit of Jethro is marked in this passage. Quickly he saw with keen insight what was wrong with Moses who was Israel's leader under God.

(1) *Responsible tasks* (vv. 13, 14). As Moses worked each day he became the judge of his people. Whenever anyone had a complaint or a grievance they brought this to the place of judicial decision. Moses was alone in this position and tried from day to day to hear all cases on behalf of his people. Their welfare and benefit was his chief concern. He was their shepherd in leadership and knew his responsibility was great before God. The trivial things of petty feuds and quarrels, the robbing of goods and jewels, the jealous disregard of personal rights, and the more serious infractions between persons came his way. If laws were broken and crimes were committed, he had to give his time and attention to give judgment and the penalty for wrong-doing as well as decide compensation for those wronged. The fullness of the law had not yet come to Israel: the nation was slowly leaving slavery

and moving into an orderly relationship as a distinctive people. Without the full writing down and crystalizing of laws, Moses had to be the law and apply it. With their background of slavery and hardship this period was now one of tension as people with freedom for the first time were easily swayed by license to do as they please. Until the Ten Commandments were known and accepted Moses alone acted to give the law as God-given to him from day to day. The Israelites were proud, fierce, and often arrogant in self-assertion and disputation.

(2) *Stress and strain* (vv. 15, 16). Modern man now knows increasingly the inevitable results of over-work and anxiety. Moses was subject to this beyond any other. All day long he served his people as a judge and the long hours wore him out physically and mentally. Perhaps he was not always aware of this, but his father-in-law Jethro saw what was taking place. His outburst is compelling and persuasive. Jethro knew human need as well as Moses. He had an insight into human nature and saw that these demands upon Moses were more than he could take. There was a limit as to what one man could endure. Weary in mind and body saw the end of the day for Moses. His powers and strength were exhausted. He said "because the people come unto me to inquire of God." Moses was the mediator between God and his nation. He alone had full knowledge of the divine will and purpose. "I make them know the statutes of God and his laws." We live in a society which says that we are supposed to know the Highway Code and expected to know the laws of the State —presumptively we are accountable. There is no excuse for anyone. Think of Moses' day without any written down law! Moses had to give the law and then interpret it. It was this state of affairs which Jethro recognized when

Moses was carried along with the pressure of the long day's work. He was concerned for Moses in his health and strength. No one individual can take the whole load for a nation. Rulers of nations; Governors of States and Provinces; and Mayors of cities today bear responsible loads in government. The strain is great and the pressures are many with the attendant long hours. Many men crack under the strain. There is one way to ease that burden and that is to have it shared. Herein lay the wisdom and foresight of Jethro.

III. His Wise Judgment in Counsel, Exodus 18:17-22

We trace in comparison the wisdom of Jethro as seen in a threefold light.

(1) *Personal responsibility.* This has been discussed largely in the previous section of this study. Out of Egypt and into the wilderness did not mean release for Moses but added burdens of office. On the march in the wilderness new problems arose from day to day and new situations demanded new decisions. Without organization and order the former slaves might erupt in lawlessness and anarchy. How to keep them in the spirit of pilgrimage and obedient to the God who had acted mightily on their behalf was a question. Until the Code of Laws had been fixed, people in distress and in tension had to have someone arbitrate and judge in their differences and claims. Exodus 25:22 tells of "the Mercy-seat in the Tabernacle from between the two cherubim which are upon the ark of the testimony, of *all things which I will give thee in commandment* unto the children of Israel," and Numbers 9:8 tells of Moses saying to them, "Stay ye, that I may hear *what Jehovah will command* concerning you." Thus from day to day and from hand-to-mouth Moses stood between

the people and God expecting God to give moment-by-moment judgment through him.

(2) *Shared responsibility*. Moving then from the personal to that which is shared by others was the counsel of Jethro to Moses. A task divided and shared can be borne easier and better. This spells out the economy of force. Wise sharing of loads will enable men to have greater reserve and strength for more tasks of life. Moses was to find this out through Jethro's counsel. In the background lay the gigantic tasks in Egypt when the Hebrew slaves were given incredible tasks to complete. Physical needs were demanding for them and now Moses had his physical needs pressing upon him. Forty years of his life had been spent in Egypt. Another forty lay behind him in Midian. Now he had entered the third forty years of his life. He was no longer a young man in the strength of youth. He had endured much over the years. Every leader must learn this—how to conserve physical and mental strength to be able to work on. Jethro told Moses, "the thing that thou doest is not good. Thou wilt surely wear away, both thou and this people that is with thee; thou are not able to perform it thyself alone. Hearken now unto my voice, I will give thee counsel, and God be with thee" (vv. 17-19a). The sagacity of Jethro is evident. Only he could speak to Moses in this way. He saw that no one man could combine in himself the work of law-giver, guide, judge, leader, and spiritual mediator of a nation.

The judgment of this man is clearly indicated as sound and practicable. He claimed to have the mind of God in this and had evidently sought divine guidance before speaking. His words are significant and searching. "Be thou for the people to Godward, and bring thou the causes to God." This implied that Moses should think of himself as the *representative* of the people before God. This carried a priestly ministry. Then, "thou shalt teach them the statutes and the laws, and shalt show them the way wherein they must walk, and the work they must do." This pointed out that Moses should conduct himself as the *mediator* of God. This gave him a prophetic ministry. Laws must be written and codified. Instruction and education should be inaugurated. Work must be provided and people shown what to do with their strength and talents. Here Moses became the lawgiver and legislator of the nation. In "bringing causes before God" lay the suggestion that only the most important items should be dealt with by him: the lesser by others.

3

Caleb,
Man of Faith and Courage

There is something clear cut about this man. Fine and honest, without any reservation, he stands out in the history of Israel as a strong character. He is associated with Joshua and together they are forever enshrined in the annals of history for their daring deeds and achievements. His father is mentioned as Jephunneh, the Kenezite. His people were on the outside of Israel and so Caleb was not directly within the chosen people's background. Along the way many foreigners or aliens were added to the elect people, and Scripture relates how these outsiders became part of the on-going story of divine providence through inter-marriage, and by deeds which were taken into the weaving of Hebrew history. Caleb was raised up under God to play his part as one who obeyed God and was associated in the partnership with Joshua at a crucial hour of history.

I. A Good Recommendation, Numbers 13:30-33
  The Israelites stood poised on the borders of the prom-

ised land with God's instructions to go in to possess that land. However, in their unbelief they wavered and Moses was ordered to send in spies to find out the condition of the land and the inhabitants before beginning the invasion (Num. 13:1, 2). The hour had come to advance but until the nation was united in its determination to move forward not much could be done. Each tribe, therefore, was requested to provide a man as part of the company of spies. Caleb represented the tribe of Judah to which he had attached himself. The twelve spies were alerted as to their duties and given all encouragement to survey the whole land and report the facts (Num. 13:17-29).

Caleb went with the others and took part in the over-all inspection of Caanan. When these spies returned two reports were given—one from the ten and another from the two, Caleb and Joshua. In orderly fashion the land was surveyed and in the reports lay two points of view. The majority recognized the great wealth of the land, but also told of the dangers involved in attacking the giants and the walled cities. Caleb and Joshua in their minority report recognized the perils to be faced, but, in the light of the potential wealth to be gained, urged that the invasion should go forward speedily. The difficulties could be met and the so-called strong inhabitants would be defeated—such was their confidence. The people rejected this minority report and began to show signs of fear and despair.

It was at this juncture that Caleb spoke up and called upon his co-patriots to go and fight and possess the land. The words of Numbers 13:30 are significant, "And Caleb stilled the people before Moses, and said, Let us go up at once, and possess it; for we are well able to overcome it." These words are in marked contrast to what the ten spies said in reply (v. 31), "But the men that went up with him said, We are not able to go up against the people; for they are stronger than we." No wonder the people, hearing this "lifted up their voice, and cried; and the people wept that night. And all the children of Israel murmured against Moses and Aaron. . ." (14:1, 2). Notice how Caleb said—"we are well able." The faint-hearted said—"we are not able." As we think of Caleb as a man of faith and courage we find in the record that this brings a good recommendation for his character and his strength. Here was no frightened man; no man given to despair; a man who had realistically taken stock of the situation. He had decided that under God's orders they should proceed to do what had been instructed. He "stilled the people" in their unrest and fear and urged the task be undertaken.

II. A Good Report, Numbers 14:1-9

The excellent witness borne by Caleb is further elaborated. Numbers 13 and 14 continue to fill in details to read and ponder. The majority report of the ten spies is labeled "an evil report" (cf. 13:32) whereas the minority report of the two was certainly "a good report" (14:7) when interpreted in the light of all the facts. The reaction of the people to the evil report was one of fear and despair and this led eventually to organizing a proposed return to Egypt. Panic, rebellion, murmuring, and weeping had taken hold of the minds of the majority. They reiterated the words "Would God that we had died in the land of Egypt! Would God, we had died in the wilderness!" This led to the wish that they should retreat back to the land of their bondage.

In the midst of this panic-filled situation, Caleb with Joshua rent his clothes—a sign that he humbled himself before God in contrition for the sorrow and the bereavement for this terrible calamity which had overtaken Israel. Moses and Aaron fell on their faces before the congregation as they pleaded with the people. Caleb is one who speaks to remind the people once more concerning the potential resources of the land ahead. Not only did he cite the facts once more about its material wealth, but he also stressed the fact that "if Jehovah delight in us, then he will bring us into this land, and give it unto us. . ." (vv. 7, 8). Here is the faith and courage of Caleb displayed once more. He speaks as a man of faith, not fear; of confidence and not cowardice; of decision and not despair. Nothing needed to spoil the plans of God according to Caleb. Had not God already shown how he had cared for and protected this nation from the days of the Exodus and through the journey thus far in the wilderness? Now on the borders of the Promised Land the prize awaited them, and in the eyes of Caleb the enemy was even then a defeated foe. He spoke of them "they are bread for us" (v. 9), a description to indicate how easy would be the victory. The defense of the enemy would crumble as bread crumbles. The word was, "fear not the people of the land, for they are *like the manna* when the shadows pass, i.e., when the sun has come out. There is then no manna left. The Lord is with us: our enemies shall melt away." Sad to say the people responded to this with "Stone him! Stone him!" (cf. v. 10) in their rebellious spirit. Caleb was not intimidated by the stones.

III. A Good Reputation, Numbers 14:11-24

The results of the rebellion of Israel at this time left God with no alternative but to chastise and punish the nation. Although Caleb and the other leaders had urged the people to heed God's word and recognize the wisdom of the invasion without delay, the evil report claimed their minds. Then it was that God ordained that Israel should now wander in the wilderness for the ensuing thirty-nine years. One year had elapsed since they came out of Egypt in the mighty Exodus. At the border of the land of promise they halt. Moses pleaded with God to remember mercy. The judgment is to be given. The sentence involved the whole nation. All who came out of Egypt would die in the wilderness. They would not enter Caanan. A new generation born in the wilderness would see the land. There were two notable exceptions—Joshua the successor to Moses as the leader to carry through the invasion; and Caleb who had stood so nobly alone against the rebellion of the people and pleaded for their obedience to God.

Verse 24 tells of God's approbation in this reservation in the midst of his judgment, "My servant Caleb, because he hath another spirit with him, and hath followed me fully, him will I bring into the land whereinto he went; and his seed shall possess it." Think of this endorsement of Caleb in God's way and time. How reassuring it must have been to have this recorded for all posterity. The nation had repudiated Caleb's report and recommendation, but his reputation in the sight of God never stood higher. In character and deed he never wavered in faith or courage. He refused to be intimidated by stones or threats and marched on with resolution in the plan of God. Caleb is "God's *servant!*" a token that God trusted him and found him trustworthy in carrying out orders. The "*spirit with him*" told of devotion and willing obedience to the will of God. He was full of confidence in the success of God's plan for Israel. He never doubted but that all enemies would be defeated. Then God said he had "*followed fully,*" a testimony and witness that the life of Caleb was that of complete surrender and devotion to God. Caleb believed that the land could be conquered. He was a man of faith. That he "wholly followed" is a Hebrew word with the picture of a ship in full sail. Caleb had no reservation and he kept nothing back in God's service. *"Him will I bring into the land"* was a pledge from God that Caleb like Joshua would be an exception to those who died in the wilderness.

From that day of rebellion and unbelief Israel went back into the wilderness; "the wilderness ended, and the temptation began; the march ended; and the wandering began" (cf. Ps. 95:10). The only record thereafter is a list of the names of the places at which they stopped, showing that time outside of God's will is lost time and wasted. All the people of twenty years and upward died in the wilderness during that next thirty-eight years. How blessed is Caleb to have the assurance then that he would yet see again the land he had surveyed and possess it.

IV. A Good Record, Joshua 14:1-13

The years pass by in the wilderness wanderings. The book of Deuteronomy describes those wanderings in review. Now the nation is ready and disciplined for that entrance so long delayed by unbelief and rebellion. Moses has gone and Joshua is the new commander and military chief. He will lead them over Jordan and the conquest will begin. In time the land will not only be taken by arms but the nation will gradually "possess their possessions." The strength of the foe and the scope of the task face the nation and as Caleb had predicted victory would come. In the campaign of conquest Joshua is prominent and little is said about Caleb until he is mentioned again in this report. What had he been doing all these years? *Waiting* for God's promise to come true! That is all.

To trace this story in detail is not simple as little is recorded. We jump to the final phase of the conquest. The land is now being divided and Caleb comes to claim his inheritance like others. In verse 14 he says, "Now therefore give me this mountain." This was a digest of what was said in the context. Caleb had kept alive in his heart the promise and pledge God had made earlier. He never wavered in his confidence that this would become true one day. In speaking of his claims to Joshua he goes over once again that day and the decision of the nation, and how he was rejected of the people because he brought a good report. Then he told how God stood by in promise to reimburse him in the pledge of the land to be his some day. All this he recounted because he had followed fully the Lord. "Jehovah hath kept me alive, as he spake, these forty and five years . . . and now, lo, I am this day fourscore and five years old" (v. 10). That was a long time to wait for God's fulfilment of his promise.

When old age looks back it finds much to chide, and to complain would be easy. Not so Caleb; he rejoices in God's faithfulness. In the eventide of his life he had come to full years. He could recall much of the history of Israel. He knew that God had led him and cared for him. His memoirs made interesting reading for the youth now around him, and if he narrated events and actions of the past how thrilling the story of the spying out of the land of promise! History was made by him and now memory brought gratitude to God for his mercies.

Here is the record of *faith* (vv. 6-8). When the tide was against him and when he stood alone he never wavered. The right supported him and nothing could thwart him in his belief. The impossible had now become actual and he stood justified. At forty years of age he had demonstrated that faith was courage and right was might. He never deviated from his duty and he never lapsed from the high calling to which he had been called. As Moses had promised the reward of faith to him, so God now confirmed the inheritance.

It was also a record of *courage* (vv. 9-11). The spirit which dared to affirm and believe is the spirit which is calm and undisturbed by changes of time and circumstances. God had kept him alive until this decisive hour and manifested his glory. God's payments come with interest although they may not be paid immediately. God kept Caleb waiting a long time but Caleb's faith was enriched. The just live by God's faithfulness and the man of faith and courage learns to live by being faithful. It was a long time since Caleb brought those grapes from the land of promise but he never forgot the place. Now God through Joshua brought fulfilment and the inheritance. Caleb is a man of blameless life and an unspotted record.

Postponements in life are difficult to take. The advance in position is delayed or seems to be postponed indefinitely. What then? Caleb worked on. He never counted the days and he did not compare his lot with others. No jealousy or bitterness entered into his heart. If he yet had the aspiration for the rewards promised he kept that in his heart. He shared in the duties of his nation in the wanderings. His people were disciplined and drilled and organized until they became as a unit and an army ready for the invasion to follow. In all this Caleb looked on and worked and dreamed and waited. He also was a man who was able to take his share of responsibility. "As yet I am as strong this day as I was in the day that Moses sent me:

as my strength was then, even so is my strength now, for war, and to go out and to come in" (v.11). Physically he might not have been as strong although mature years could well claim to be, but he had the indomitable strength of spirit without which a man of war fights in vain. He did not ask for an easy place as he said he would take the hill country at Hebron where, he recalled, dwelt some of the mighty men, the giants, and the great walled and fortified cities of the enemy" (v. 12). Confidence in God led him to say he would drive out the enemy.

This is a record of *expectation* (vv. 12-13). Hope as we have seen was supreme in Caleb's life. He had waited for over forty years for the opportunity to demonstrate that he was right and that God was on the side of those who fully trusted in him. God's delays are not necessarily his denials. Caleb was a veteran soldier but he was skilled in the ways of warfare. His inheritance he claimed but he stood ready to fight for it like anyone else!

V. A Good Reward, Joshua 14:14, 15

The last picture is that of the old soldier entering into his possessions in peace. The Jordan was crossed; the battle was fought; Israel began the subjugation of the land. Later, in Judges 1:20, it tells how Caleb took Hebron and drove out the giants left there. Joshua's record in these verses record that Caleb received his reward for faithful service well done. The reason is given in that he "wholly followed Jehovah, the God of Israel." Several times we have found these words in his story. They might well sum up his life and character. Here was a young man who early gave his all to God and in absolute devotion to his will found the plan for his life and work. When beset by difficulties and opposed by forces which hindered he nevertheless did not waver in his purpose. His reward is here for his record is good. He spoke out for the truth when it was unpopular. He stood alone when the crowd was swayed by other forces of evil. He never asked for an easy life, and in the reward given he would not receive it without first giving his share of strength for the defeat of the enemy.

At eighty-five years of age Caleb is no longer the young intrepid soldier ready for a commando encounter with the enemy. He might well have retired honorably but there still throbs within him the spirit to venture and he is ready to draw his sword once more. "Old soldiers never die" is a word that does not need its other line for completion in this case—Caleb would be there at the finish and in the fight to the last. He seemed to have the secret of youth perpetual as he stood to take over his inheritance. When the ten spies gave their evil report they saw God through their difficulties and he seemed small. Caleb with Joshua had seen their difficulties through God and God was great and almighty.

There are fortified cities of evil to be taken and entrenched giants to fight in our day. In the moral and spiritual warfare we may well be encouraged by Caleb in faith and courage. In youth and in mature years the same spirit can prevail for victory. Caleb never knew what it was to despair or quit!

4

Gideon,
Foe of Paganism

The thrilling story of this young man who rose to become the head of the nation is one that stirs the imagination and captures our minds. When deeds of danger are done and when victories are won against superior forces we are prone to hero-worship. The exploits of Gideon are forever enshrined in history for all to learn that a minority with God is more than a match for the battalions ranged against it. This is the heart of Gideon's story. Leaders are always wanted in every nation. Where shall they be found? There are the usual schools and training centers for those who prepare in law, medicine, government, and in military skill. Once in a while a man is thrown up from lesser levels of privilege to demonstrate that natural endowments may tip the scale in selecting an outstanding leader. Our age is attracted by "men of distinction" for the higher posts of leadership, but out of every level of society and from the lesser privileged people come those who make their contribution far beyond what men have dreamed of. Such was Gideon who was no weakling, but who exemplified the best traits of leadership in courage and devotion. Although at first he was retiring in disposition and hesitant; when the call came to serve his country, he was ready.

I. A Man of the Soil, Judges 6:1-32

Gideon lived in the period of the Book of Judges. It was a wild, tempestuous time. Lawless deeds prevailed and "every one did that which was right in his own eyes" (Judg. 17:6). This was anarchy and selfishness in command. After the time of the settlement of Israel in the promised land came this unrest and turmoil. Described as "the iron age" the rebellious spirit of evil seemed to break down the former sanctities of life and make Israel idolatrous.

(1) *Selected by God* (vv. 1-25a). The background of Gideon's life is that of a farmer. His father Joash was of the tribe of Manasseh. During this time the Midianites had over-run the land and for seven years there was bondage and trouble. The cycle was clear in Israel's checkered career—*rebellion, retribution, repentance,* and *restoration.* Because they "did evil in the sight of the Lord" (6:1), the consequences are clearly marked. Then they "cried unto Jehovah because of Midian" (6:7) and this followed, "Israel was brought very low because of Midian" (6:6). God heard that cry for deliverance and in remembrance of his covenant sent Israel a deliverer or judge or savior as he was called. Sin brought its servitude; then they cried in supplication for help; and finally God sent them salvation by way of a savior he had selected.

Gideon is one of the deliverers raised up by God in an hour of national crisis. He came from the farm and the plough. He was a young man when God chose him for this task. He came from an ordinary family of lesser privilege and without any outstanding background. His people and he had suffered at the hands of Midian and he knew the constant dread of the enemy pouncing upon them. He was not a mighty man and certainly not the kind to be selected by the vote of his fellows (cf. I Cor. 1:26—"not many noble, not many mighty are called").

The messenger of God came to him when he was working (vv. 11-18). The salutation embodied all that he was yet to be. Here is the paradox of the truth—"Gideon was beating out wheat . . . . Jehovah is with thee, thou mighty man of valor." A farmer does not suggest the picture of a soldier! God here revealed that he was to become what he was not. Oliver Cromwell in England is not unlike this in his experience. The farmer who worked strenuously was physically strong and with his daily contact with nature clear in mind and eye for any task. The occasion here found Gideon in a cave secretly working at the wheat, having saved it from the enemy. The place and circumstances speak of poverty and abject subjection in a time of depression. Gideon's reply demonstrates how low in spirit he was and how desperate the times. He tells that his family is the poorest; that he is the least in that family; and how could he save Israel? (v. 15). Yet God promised his presence, "I will be with thee" (v. 16). Gideon asked for a sign to be sure of the divine favor that this was no mere dream on his part. The fire which consumed the cakes followed (vv. 19-24) and Gideon knew that Jehovah was there and that he had been given audience with God. He, therefore, erects an altar for a memorial, called "Jehovah-shalom," the God of peace.

(2) *Tested by God* (vv. 25b-27). Gideon had asked proof from God about this call and now he is tried out by God

in what follows. A daring deed was demanded. To go into the neighboring community where the Midianites held supremacy and there destroy their religious center of worship. Knowing now that God had called him through the fiery test in the cave he is sent on this mission of destruction. God would test him in return. This required an act of obedience on the part of Gideon. Gideon was no coward but he had acted in the only way one could act in the light of the situation—he would not act unless God had given him a sign and seal of his approval.

It seems that his father was the one who had succumbed to the seductions of the enemy through their religion. He had an altar to Baal and it was this altar Gideon was asked to destroy. God will not have as a leader of the nation a man who tolerated idolatry or compromised with evil. This was the next step for Gideon in preparation for his mission to come. Baal worship was unclean and corrupting. Gideon took ten men with him to help in the breaking down of the pagan center of worship. Imagine the state of mind of Gideon—young, modest, retiring, and knowing he is one of lesser-privileged men of the time—and God asking, yes, God saying he has been selected to do this—and we realize how incredulous it all seemed! Yet he moves forward into this task that night. Baal had led astray many in Israel and as a religion gave the people license to indulge in immoral deeds and dances which debauched them. The Baalim thrived in association with fertility rites and the land, and Israel had that in common. Jehovah was an opposite kind of God demanding righteousness and morality. Would Gideon destroy that which lay at the center of Israel's life? Here was the supreme test even as God called him—and he responded!

(3) *Approved by God* (vv. 28-32). Tests reveal character.

God allowed this. The people of that area resented what he did. They demanded the death of Gideon. This was a threat which could mean the end of the enterprize begun in faith. Having thrown down the Baal altar he erected one for Jehovah. It is easy to destroy: it is more difficult to build. Construction is a test as well as destruction. The quality of his faith and conviction was such that he was the foe of paganism. He stood for spiritual worship. There are still bad religions and idolatry around us today. Cruelty, superstition, injustice, uncleanness, as well as the gods of money and success without moral values—the Christian should not only tear down but also replace with the Christian standards.

Gideon received his new name at this time—Jerubaal, or "let Baal contend"—suggesting that Gideon was the champion of the true God who won the victory over entrenched evil and vested interests. God's approval of Gideon came at the place where it was most difficult for him to show his faith—at home. The false god was destroyed at the heart of Israel's life and home. A demonstration had been made in a practical way so that people were convinced that this lowly, untrained, unasked young man was now God's servant for some destiny. Who works on our behalf? Gideon's deeds convinced all that God works on behalf of those who trust in him. Thus God endorsed Gideon's acts of faith and became the champion of the hour. Reform began at home and God approved his man of valor.

II. A Man of the Spirit, Judges 6:33-40

Gideon had been told he was "a man of valor" (v 12) and although he may not have thought of himself in that category, he had just seen how God enabled him to achieve the impossible. A further experience now came to him.

(1) *His need is obvious.* Although called to this high and exalted position of leadership in the nation, still Gideon must have had reservations. What strength did he have? What skills were his? He had his mandate to serve God but where would he get the mastery of the evils around him? He faced fighting against Midianites but he had to uproot idolatry first. Having taken that first step against idolatry he now awaited his next step. Here God came upon him in a remarkable manner in the Spirit of God. "The Spirit of God *came* upon Gideon; and he blew a trumpet" (v. 34). The original word suggests that the Spirit of God *clothed himself with* Gideon. This could mean that God came upon Gideon as a robe is put around a person (this is the general interpretation) which would mean the "coming upon" was a clothing of the man by an invisible cloak. The other (and more unusual meaning) interpreta-tion is that the Spirit of God came to indwell the person of Gideon. This would anticipate the fuller revelation of the New Testament where the Spirit came upon the disci-ples of Christ and now indwells each one as the very presence of the Christ Himself. What is now for every believer was the experience in Old Testament times for selected individuals—Gideon especially. Thus he is given honor as a robe suggests distinction and position in leader-ship. He is clothed as by a coat of mail or armor to defend himself in battle.

(2) *His opportunity is clear.* Immediately Gideon is in a fight against Midian. His only preparation then is this spiritual gift of unusual fortitude for fight. The man of valor will now exercise a strength beyond his own. He asks another sign from God in the changing fleece so that he is convinced once and for all that he may venture forth

as the leader of the forces of liberation in his nation. Having received the enduement of the Holy Spirit he "blew a trumpet." This marked out the practical nature of the spiritual experience. He rallied his friends and neighbors to fight for freedom. He called for volunteers. He asked for sacrifices to be made. Abiezer, once against him, now rallied. Men of Dan and Naphtali in the remote places of the land came to his aid. Gideon in blowing the trumpet anticipated victory before engaging the enemy. The ordinary man had become extraordinary in moral and spiritual strength. The untried and untrained farmer had now become a leader of soldiers. The undisciplined became a dedicated force and ready to fight. Fear gave way to faith and the heart became brave and ready to meet the impossible odds. Always the men of the Spirit are the men of action in the decisive hour.

III. A Man of the Sword, Judges 7:1—8:21

Gideon is the hero of an age-long story and a victory which turned the tide of history.

(1) *Sifting the ranks* (7:1-8). Before Gideon could be sure that all who rallied to his banner would be able to fight as he intended and planned he had to test them. No doubt he was surprised and yet pleased when after the blowing of the trumpet as a signal for Israel's fighting men to come he could count up to thirty-two thousand. That was a formidable army, but this was not what God had planned. The first test was an appeal to their fear. Fear plays an important part in life. We are swayed by our emotions and fear is one of the strongest. At once twenty-two thousand men left when confronted with the threat of battle and the fierceness of the opposition. That left ten thousand would-be fighters. Again, God demanded an-

other test and this time in their habit of drinking at the water. Those who lapped like a dog by putting their hand to their mouth were placed apart, while the others who went down on their knees were separated from them. The latter nine thousand, seven hundred were then sent home and *the three hundred* left became the fighting men under Gideon. God saw how untrustworthy would be those thousands who carelessly indulged under the lure of the flesh, over against the three hundred who exemplified a spirit of vigilence and disciplined life in the spirit. Thus were selected the strong and resolute, the men who could be trusted under rigorous conditions, those who did not think of themselves before the enemy's unexpected assault. This is ever the divine principle of selection for service. As Gideon, so the church in this day is served well by the minority group ready and vigilant. In devotion no risks are taken while we watch the issues of the day. Quality is preferred to quantity. God wins his victories not by numbers but by the few and men like Gideon.

(2) *Surprising the enemy* (7:9-25). Gideon's strategy given by God is remarkable in its daring and planning. It's execution was carried through without mishap. The advance spying-out of the enemy is thrilling to the imagination. Then follows the actual battle. The weapons used were not the usual ones—swords *and* trumpets! The latter brought fear and dismay to the aroused Midianites and the former smote their enemies to rout and death. The Battle of Jezreel is recorded as a divine victory to show how the powers of God are superior to the forces of evil. The victory was one of faith over natural forces. God had selected the best men to fight, and in their obedience to Gideon's commands the campaign was soon over. Gideon might have had his moments of misgiving for such an

undertaking, but when God allowed him to visit the Midianite camp during the night he saw and heard that which reassured him (cf. vv. 10, 11, 13, 15).

(3) *Securing the victory* (8:1-21). During that battle the pitchers were broken with their torches; the trumpets were blown; and the shout of victory was heard with the sword in hand. Matthew Henry quaintly says that Gideon contrived to strike a terror upon this army, and so put them to confusion—"with a great noise; with a great blaze; and with a great shout." Men fought that day for their land and their homes and families, but most of all "for the Lord and for Gideon" as the *sword* stood as the symbol of all that was done. As a man of the sword Gideon had also to pacify the Ephraimites who made trouble for him because they were not allowed to fight. He also had to discipline others who refused his men help in their pursuit of the enemy. Gideon had internal difficulties before he saw the final stage of his long campaign ended and the land at rest.

IV. A Man of Salvation, Judges 8:22-35

The final stage of this story is that Gideon is asked to become the "savior" or "judge" of the nation (v. 22). His first reaction is a refusal "I will not rule over you. . . . Jehovah shall rule over you." As a Theocracy, Israel knew only the rule of God but now came signs of decline from the highest and best as they began to defect from divine rule and sought a king eventually. Relief in the midst of rebellion and decline came as God allowed them to have Judges and fourteen in all served the nation. Gideon refused to be as a king and this is to his credit. He saw the implications and he would not usurp God's place over the nation. He demonstrated a humble spirit in not allow-

ing the clamor of the crowd to crown him. He recognized
the implications of divine sovereignty. He knew his place
as a servant.

Gideon ruled for forty years and Israel knew the leadership of the soldier. Oliver Cromwell in England having
won his battles with his "three hundred" ironsides then
ruled with strength. It was natural for the people to seek
the war-hero to be their leader. But there were perils in
high office which were not found in the field of battle.
Although he refused to be king, Gideon was not averse
to asking a reward—simple though it seemed at the time—
"give me the earrings of his prey." He took these from his
men and made an ephod and put it in the city of Ophra.
This thing became a snare and an idol so that the people
sought after it as a god. This was Gideon's mistake and
sin. The great soldier had his faults—he little realized the
power of sin. At the beginning of his career he had destroyed the altar of Baal, and now at the end he allows
idolatry to creep in a little. He compromised with evil.
The kingly garment (ephod) studded with gold made
from earrings became the symbol of evil. An altar was
built for it and idolatry ensued.

Gideon never coveted honors for himself. He lived
simply and desired nothing for his family line in high
office. He also did wrong in multiplying wives and transgressed the law. This was another phase of a strong, resolute man who had his weaknesses of the flesh. He who did
so much for Israel and was obedient to God in the day of
the ordeal is now seen at the last as a weak and failing old
man. In the ripeness of the years he loses his strength
through lack of discipline and devotion. He allows com-
promising things to intrude into his life and the life of his
people. The spoils of victory proved to be too seductive

to him. He who could take his army to war had no skill to fight a private battle with an unseen enemy. He had lost the sense of the divine strategy in this final fight for his soul!

Gideon is the hero of history who was the foe of paganism. He routed the enemies of his country, but he failed to win the final victory in his heart. His greatness is tarnished. His end is under a cloud. *And* yet who shall say that he did not serve God in his day and generation in spite of personal failure? God worked through this man in spite of his frailty of clay. When his life was remembered men kindly thought of his goodness (v. 35) to Israel.

Ruth,

A Foreigner, Who Won Her Way

All the world responds to a love story. This is seen in the literature of the ages and in the stories which are well-known. The Bible has its share of these. Among the sweetest and choicest is that of Ruth for her mother-in-law Naomi. The period when this took place lay in the time of the book of the Judges. Israel had taken possession of the land of promise. Their leaders were men raised up as saviors or judges in a time of political and social transition. Behind lay the slavery of Egypt and the wanderings in the wilderness. Before them lay the settled life of becoming a nation with its organization and government. A movement had started to have a king like other nations and no longer be ruled simply under God, as in a theocracy. During this interim period there was much unrest and open rebellion. The time has been well described as "the iron age" when lawlessness and anarchy abounded. People did what they liked and refused to be governed by moral and spiritual laws. Idolatry and immorality were rife. Strife and confusion shook the social and domestic life of the people. The times were bad and the outlook was dark. Just when it seemed darkest there bloomed this idyllic story of love and purity. Amid the foul stench of evil came this sweet odor of true love and devotion. In the miasma and smog of darker days came the bright light of dawning hope. It is as if one stumbled in the grime of a coal mine and suddenly found at his feet a white lily growing. Dust might be all around but the petals of this flower would be clean and untouched. This is the story of Ruth.

I. Ruth's Background, 1:1-10

In its literary form this is a pastoral idyll. Outstanding in its rustic setting it speaks of pastoral beauty. When a group of intellectuals gathered on one occasion in Paris they discussed great literature and at the same time seemed to disparage anything deeply religious. One of the guests was Benjamin Franklin who asked permission to read something he had found. They listened to the simple tale which he brought to them. They were thrilled and moved and some asked what it was and where it was to be found. They had not heard anything like it for its sheer beauty of language, its imaginative description, and its idyllic grace. He told them this was the Book of Ruth from The Bible!

Ruth is the "heathen" young woman, a stranger to Israel, one born as a Moabitess, a foreigner. The map will indicate how near Moab was to Palestine and yet how far removed the people were in their religion and standards of life. However, it was in this background that Ruth was born and lived. Her association with Israel came through marriage. The famine in the land of Palestine led two young men and their parents to leave home and seek help in this foreign land. There they settled and intermarried. They came from the family of Elimelech and Naomi; their names were Mahlon and Chilion. In the land of their adoption Elimelech died leaving Naomi a widow. Then her two sons found wives, Orpah and Ruth. After ten years these two men died leaving the two young widows with their mother-in-law. Three graves in this new land had wounded the heart of Naomi and she came to the decision that the exiled heart would find rest in returning home. The chords of memory were strong and she realized that in widowhood and loneliness this would be the best.

This background also touched Ruth, the heroine of the story. We trace here how circumstances can change a life. The days were difficult in that politically and socially there was unrest and anarchy. There was a famine in the land of Palestine and this had brought Naomi and her sons into the life of Moab. Moab then was a place of security and ease. Naomi's sons married outside the pale. The law ordered the Israelite to marry only within the covenant relation and here these two young men compromised their standards. We must see later how God over-ruled this in Ruth's choice. The uncertainty of life is reflected here in the death of the sons of Naomi and the fact that the young widows were childless. Transient and fleeting were the joys of marriage. A widow's lot then was one of desolation and no promise of future comfort.

II. Ruth's Choice, 1:11-19

This came in the hour of sorrow and bereavement. Her mother-in-law had decided to return to Palestine. Good-byes were being said and the parting of the ways had come. Naomi urged her daughters-in-law to leave her and stay in their own home. There was weeping and sadness in parting. Orpah chose then to go back and the inference is that she returned to resume her old life in Moab with its social customs and its idolatry (v. 15). The kiss of farewell was given by Orpah but Ruth "clave to her mother-in-law" (v. 14). There was something lacking in Moab. She knew instinctively that Naomi reflected other standards and another kind of life. She had been influenced by her marriage and the decision of Naomi. There was evidently affection and trust between these two women. Naomi had a sense of duty and a loyalty to her people and her native land. Now that conditions had changed she felt she should return. In this was her religious conviction under the covenant of God. Affliction had not hardened her heart.

Ruth was not forced into this choice or persuaded by Naomi. Naomi tried to give her the opportunity to return to her own land and people. There is a discussion which ends in this final irrevocable decision for Ruth. She will go with Naomi. Then follows those memorable words which have touched the hearts of multitudes: "Intreat me not to leave thee, and to return from following after thee; for wither thou goest, I will go; and where thou lodgest, I will lodge; thy people shall be my people, and thy God my God" (v. 16). "Where thou diest, will I die, and there will I be buried: Jehovah do so to me, and more also, if aught but death part thee and me" (v. 17). This resolution is forever enshrined in the literature that can never pass away. It is most moving in spirit and gracious in expression. Its feeling and depth are allied in words of beauty and dignity.

The choice embodies a vow and resolution. Naomi did not have any asylum or security to give to Ruth, yet Ruth spoke with faith and confidence that it would be so. The lot of a widow or young woman was precarious in the East and only in marriage was there the basis of sanctuary. To travel, to rest, and to join her life in the strange land with

another people took faith and courage. At the foundation
of this gesture lay a committal to the Hebrew God and
religion. She swore as by an oath that nothing could shake
her from this avowal. She has become a convert to the life
and faith of the covenant people. Naomi saw that Ruth
was stedfast and convinced without wavering. "So they
two went" (v. 19). Thus Ruth turned her back upon the
past with its grief and sorrow, its idols and superstition.
The arrival is not without its pathos for "all the city of
Bethlehem was moved" (v. 19) and "they said, is this
Naomi?" (v. 19). The latter is in the Hebrew feminine—
the women of the city said this. Her intimate friends
gathered to see and to talk. What stir and questions as
these women questioned and discussed the days of yester-
day, Naomi's experiences, and now this new, young
woman with her! Little did they think she was destined
to play a part in history of great eventualities.

III. Ruth's Opportunities, 2:1-13

How striking the story is told—"in the beginning of the
barley-harvest" (1:22). That was the providence of God.
Just at that particular time the women came to Bethlehem.
This was the first of the regular harvests, the wheat harvest
following. The romance of a true love story follows. Boaz
is a kinsman of Naomi and he is spoken of here as "a
mighty man of wealth," "a valiant hero"—thus came the
meeting of Ruth and Boaz. As in every society there are
rich people and sometimes poor relations. One branch of
a family is different from another, yet they have to recognize the ties of blood and kinship. Here was the opportunity for Naomi to arrange for her daughter-in-law to
work in the field of Boaz and find shelter and remunera-
tion to help the two women. God works through the

natural order, and incidents that seem incidental become historic and important.

The two women had come back to poverty but in that circumstance was to be the solution of their needs. Humble and honest toil are honored by God and no life is outside of his care and love. The willing spirit of Ruth is evidenced in this and she gleans much more eventually than just corn. There is another reaping and harvesting to follow. Thus does God prepare the soul for his best and choicest gifts. The Levitical law allowed that a stranger should be allowed to glean in the harvest field, following the reaper. "Her hap was to light on a part of the field belonging to Boaz" (v. 3). The *hap* is no chance or luck or accident—the word suggests something happening within a purpose. The accidental becomes providential; the *casual* is seen to be *causal*; and God is found in every detail working out his plan for her. This leads to Boaz finding her and giving his moral and practical protection to her in the midst of perils she would scarce imagine.

Gleaning (vv. 8, 9) was a common practice in that day and it was the courtesy of the Hebrew people to give some thought to the stranger and the foreigner who might be in need. The poor were not overlooked. The Israelite was reminded in this gesture that once, he, too, had been an alien and an exile in slavery and in another land. To show kindness within their gates was encouraged. Harvest time was a busy time for all, and some workers might be boorish and rude to a stranger and even insulting to a modest young woman. The kindness of Boaz was her safeguard and he was given honor and respect. Thus she found her way of toil lightened with kindness and food provided for her and Naomi. Many displaced persons in modern days have come to our country out of Europe and Asia to find homes and work as they begin a new life for themselves and their children. Christians within the fellowship of their church have provided money and materials so that the foreigner and the exile might start afresh and share in our plenty.

Kindness (vv.10-13) was also of the essence of the spiritual faith enjoined upon the Hebrew. Boaz was a man of this spirit. The relation of master and laborer is now seen as something fine in those difficult days. In contrast to much of the impersonal ways of our technological and automotive age it is refreshing to go back to this early relationship rarely found today. Then was the old-time salutation of Boaz the master to his men and women who worked for and with him, the courteous greeting and the close relation between them. We have lost much in the machine age that was a healthy respect for one another in the pastoral setting of Boaz and Ruth. Ruth was shown much kindness. "Why have I found grace in thine eyes? . . .let me find favor in thy sight" (vv. 11-13). This is the note of grace.

The compassion and protection of Boaz on behalf of Ruth is one of the touching and sensitive stories in all literature. All that happened was no accident, as we trace afterwards. Within the providence of God seemingly trivial events have relation to the over-all plan of God. He works in the human affairs of everyday life. He is not a God removed from our mundane interests. No life seeking divine help and the will of God as supreme will be disappointed in this light. Even the kindness done to some stranger may make the difference between light and darkness, salvation or defeat.

IV. Ruth's Reward, 3:1—4:12

The love that Boaz had for Ruth developed from his care and concern for a strange young woman who was also related to him by family ties, though distant. Gradually he came to love her even as he had to face the demands of the Levitical Law concerning his next-of-kin who died leaving a widow without a child to continue the family line. Here again is the wisdom of ancient laws providing for the on-going purpose of the race, and especially God's plan for the coming of the Messiah-Redeemer. Boaz thus brought her into this closer relationship with the people of God. He turned out to be the *Goel*, the Kinsman-Redeemer as well as the master of the harvest in which she labored. "The Lord recompense thy work" (2:12) had greater meaning than simply food.

What followed in the harvest time is not to be construed as immoral or unwise. Some have thought so and yet we must see these events in the light of the rough and rude age in which they occurred. There was also Hebrew custom which evidently allowed such an occurrence. Ruth had worked a while under the eye of Boaz and he had come to know her. He had also sensed the relationship she had to him as the next of kin. If no one else would come forward to give her the right of the widow in Israel, then he could. Perhaps he delayed or hesitated and in her intuitive manner Naomi encouraged Ruth to carry out this act of going to the feet of Boaz at night so that he might find her there seeking his loving protection. She was not an impure woman and dressed with care so that she was not mistaken for a loose woman who was a harlot. He was an honorable man of rectitude and understanding. The crucial hour of their meeting under these circumstances led to the action

of Boaz to take up her case. "Shall I not seek rest for thee?
(3:1). Such *rest* was the Menuchah of the Hebrew language and custom. This was the word for the husband's
home and protection. This was the place of honor and
freedom for a woman.

In addition to the Menuchah of rest there was also the
relation of the *Goel* or Kinsman-Redeemer. The unloos-
ing of one who was bound and who is restored to her high
position was done by someone paying a price. In Israel
when a man died without issue, his brother, or nearest of
kin, was bound to marry his widow. This was based on the
conviction that life was the greatest treasure of a people.
Thus the Goel redeemed his brother's name from being
blotted out. Our Lord Jesus Christ, later, is the world's
Kinsman-Redeemer. Boaz acted on behalf of Ruth and her
husband who had died and took her to be his wife.

Boaz's next step was to go to the gate of the city where
the ancient ritual of the kinsman was carried out. Here
the judges sat, either in public or in one of the rooms
above the arch of the gates. There Boaz was able to enact
what was right and required of him. When a man took
over land he planted his foot on the soil and thus symbol-
ized his possession. Taking off a shoe in this case implied
that he refused the possession and gave it to the one
willing to receive it—in this case, Ruth.

V. Ruth's Recompense, 4:13-22

The consequences of these acts by Ruth and by Boaz
had far-reaching results. Their marriage followed and in
the joy of their union Boaz became the father of a child.
Ruth as mother would little realize that this son Obed was
destined to be the living link in the continuation of the

family which would eventually bring the Messiah. "Obed begat Jesse, and Jesse begat David" (v. 22). A simple summing up of the Book of Ruth and yet how astounding! David became king in Israel and laid the foundations of Messianic promises. What had been pledged by God in the Covenant to Abraham was later confirmed in the Covenant to David (cf. Matt. 1:5-16; Luke 3:22-32). Christ in the fulness of time becomes the Rest-giver (the Menuchah of the world) and the Goel or Kinsman-Redeemer. In the story of Ruth we see the hand of God working out his plan and purpose, ever finding a willing servant to do his will. Men may fail or try to thwart God but in his providence and sovereign love he makes history to be the instrument of his salvation.

Ruth who at the first knew only an alien culture and idolatrous religion; who knew the sorrow and bitterness of widowhood; and who chose to become an exile and foreigner in a strange land was recompensed by God in his choice of her as an ancestor of the Messiah. Thus it is that in the Genealogy of Matthew's Gospel concerning the Christ is the name of Ruth—a foreigner in the royal line of the King of kings! This is the grace and love of God which is shown when Christians respect the alien and love the stranger for Christ's sake. We never know what will result from this gesture of gracious action. Ruth made her choice—many make their choice of work or study. Some make their choice of a life-partner—how important this is. Choice is made concerning friends but most of all concerning God and Christ. America is a land where aliens and foreigners have come to build a new world "a nation under God." Here we are all Americans who pledge allegiance to its flag and laws. Christians dare not refuse the same privileges to others who choose in the spirit of Ruth—"Thy people shall be my people." Best of all is when the alienated from God say "Thy God shall be my God." In that we find, like Ruth, rest and redemption.

6

Hannah,
A Woman Who Kept Her Promise

The women of the Bible stand out in their unexpected contribution to life and work. Men in general dominate the record as they are the majority in the events of history. But God has taken note of the women who have their part to play. A few like Rahab and the women who washed the feet of Christ are socially outcasts, but the majority of those whose names and deeds are preserved are women of good character and gracious spirit. Such an one is Hannah. She, like Ruth, arises in a time of difficulty for Israel and is another providential link in the on-going purpose of God. When that nation was passing through its readjustment from being a horde of slaves to becoming an organized body, Hannah stands out as the mother of Samuel the prophet who led the nation into a new day. Within the first two chapters of I Samuel is found all we know about her in thirteen verses. Yet this woman was a willing instrument of God. God passed by some of the great and the mighty for his purpose. From time to time God worked through a woman and mothers have been used for divine ends.

I. The Saddened Wife, 1:1-8

This is a sad picture of a home where there is sorrow and provocation. The Hebrews had a reverence and respect for marriage and family life, so that this incident stands out in all its somber hue of disappointment and fretting.

(1) *Her marriage is honorable.* She is the wife of Elkanah, an Ephraimite. He was a Levite and came from an honorable background. He was devout and regular in attendance at worship. Domestically he had done a wrong to Hannah. He had taken a second wife, a common practice in those days. Perhaps he meant well when Hannah herself did not have any children. Like Abraham and Jacob earlier he might have thought he did his name a service in this. Every Hebrew sought to have a family and his name continued in honor. However, in his second wife he had transgressed the original command of God concerning marriage. Mischief resulted and her motherhood caused strife and jealousy between the two wives. The second wife "provoked" Hannah, an indication of the tension within the home. She was able to bear children whereas at this time Hannah was childless. Nothing but unhappiness came to Elkanah and his home. As for Hannah she endured all this knowing that her marriage had been one of honor and love.

(2) *Her childlessness is disappointing.* To a Hebrew woman to be without a child was a sore trial. It looked to her and to her friends as if God had forsaken her. Barrenness was difficult to take for motherhood was a sacred experience for a woman. The family was the unit of the

nation, and through motherhood came the perpetuation of the race and especially God's purpose for Israel. Others than Hannah knew this strange tension within the family in similar situations e.g., Sarah, Rebekah, Rachel, Manoah's wife, and later Elisabeth (Luke 1:7). This state was thought of as a misfortune as the highest religious ideals blessed the fruitful woman. When the mothers of Israel were without child at first it seemed that only the divine intervention brought them children, and this showed God's special concern for this people. Naturally a son guaranteed that the tribe or family continued in name and posterity. The first-born belonged to God (Num. 3:44). Later, the Jewish mother hoped that she might bear the Messiah promised of God.

(3) *Her sorrow is heart-rending.* No doubt she was grieved that her womanhood was not completed in this final expectancy of sexual life and love. She thought she had failed her husband in this union in marriage. Her rival provoked her and caused her more grief and pain. Frustrated and forlorn she knew herself to be. Added to this would be that she loved children and ardently desired a child in her mother instinct. Polygamy brought lowered standards and Hannah felt this keenly as though she had failed her husband. Elkanah, to his credit, is seen as a man who loves Hannah with a true and sincere affection. He shows his love in the gifts he brings. He remembers her with "a double portion" usually reserved for the most honored person at a meal. He did all he could to reassure her that she had the premier place in his home and love. He maintained his religious devotion before the Lord and in every way sought to ease Hannah's burden. But she lost her appetite and gave way to constant weeping in her sorrow of heart. Her only compensation was

that her husband completed her life in devotion and love.

II. The Solemn Vow, 1:9-11

The domestic situation is not easily resolved until a day of crisis comes when Hannah is determined to do something unusual and in desperation seeks a way out of her trouble.

(1) *Prayer is offered.* In this lay the suggestion not of one prayer but that out of constant praying came this special prayer. Like Hannah we pray in general terms and pray for much, but there can come a time when we concentrate and think only of one petition. Then follows perseverance and patience. The spirit of persistent prayer is such that God commends. The prayer that is here is one that is characterized by "bitterness of soul and weeping sore." The intense spirit and concern is noted and this provides the background for the words of the prayer. Prayer is varied in spirit and occasion and the use of language. In this first chapter of Samuel the original word suggests prayer which is that of intercession and petition. It comes from the idea of asking God to arbitrate in a judicial manner concerning this case. In addition to this is I Samuel 2:1 where Hannah is in the House of God after the birth of Samuel and she continues to pray. The same word is used but in the sense of a liturgical prayer of poetic fervor. This spoke of constancy and persistence but directed prayer.

Hannah's prayer was childlike and in faith. She was a woman demanding something which had been denied her in nature up to this time. She was baffled in her agony of soul and pleaded with God. Here was no ordinary prayer of trite words and careful phrasing. The flood-gates of the heart were opened and she is urgent and persistent. The one thing in her mind was for the gift of a child. Only those who have been baffled and perplexed can know the pathos of this prayer of Hannah's. Some might think this a prayer which was selfish but this is not so recalling the background of the Hebrew woman and the nation's future. The conditions were difficult in the nation with spiritual leadership at a low ebb. The times required a strong leader and God must send one soon if Israel is to survive. Did Hannah dream that a child of her's might be a leader?

(2) *A vow is pledged.* To take or make a vow is an act of dedication to God. It involved the pledge of future devotion. There was a binding force beyond measure to do the will of God at all costs. Sacrifice was implied in this. The language of this vow is moving in its intensity. Hannah frustrated and sore of heart, sorrowful and wistful, vexed and fatigued by tension, is desperate before God. Emotion and urgency find expression in this vow. The "man-child" she asks for she pledges in return to be a dedicated man to Jehovah all his life. She will not keep this child for herself. She will act as guardian and nurse to train the child for the service of God. Even before he is conceived and born she sees in imagination the coming of one who will more than fulfil all these desires of her heart before God. He would not only be dedicated and separated to God, but "no razor would come upon his head." This related to the Nazarite vow of dedication. We have no evidence that Samuel later was a Nazarite but in his prophet's vocation he exemplified the same sense of calling.

III. The Satisfied Wife, 1:12-18

Immediately after the prayer and vow of Hannah comes the reaction on the part of Eli who witnessed her impassioned gesture in the House of God. How did this appear to others?

(1) *Silent prayer.* Eli's reaction at first was to think of Hannah as a woman who was drunk. She was so moved and under an emotional strain that she prayed with strong crying and tears. She staggered with her sorrow. Although she prayed in public her prayer was private in that no sound was heard. Secretly, only God knew what she desired. The ancient tabernacle had become a small temple and here the priest came at his hours of service. He saw the woman in her emotional upheaval of soul but did not recognize this at first for what it was. He was soon corrected as Hannah poured out before him her sense of loss and desire. His own sons were shamelessly guilty of consorting with drunken women near God's house and possibly he might have assumed Hannah was one of them. He should have known better. A drunken person is usually noisey. She was silent. Thus she "continued praying before Jehovah."

(2) *Promised answer.* Eli after listening to Hannah spoke only those words she longed to hear. She was assured that her prayer would be answered by God. Eli encouraged her devotion and gave her the priestly blessing "go in peace." He might not know the particular petition she offered but he could endorse her spirit of importunity and perseverance. To all that he could say "amen." He added, "the God of Israel grant thee thy petition that thou hast asked of him." His spirit was so attuned in spiritual insight and knowledge that he could desire this for this woman who worshipped and who prayed with such intensity of devotion. With the assurance of answered prayer the change in Hannah was most marked. She went home that day "and her countenance was no more sad." Elkanah saw it at once

and rejoiced with his wife in this new day that had dawned
for them both. She also resumed taking food, and husband
and wife next morning went back to God's house there to
worship. What mingled emotions for Elkanah as well as
for Hannah. What affection and devotion welled up in
their hearts at God's goodness to them! The prayer was
answered in good time and Hannah knew she would bear
a son. Thus Samuel came. "The Lord remembered her"
may well sum up this part of the story. She had prayed
"If Thou wilt. . .give. . .I will give" (v.11). With that
prayer and vow all selfish desire in petition was removed.
Mothers who believe that "children are a heritage of the
Lord" are those who have this spirit of dedication.

IV. The Sacred Obligation, 1:20-28
Now begins the carrying out of all that Hannah had
promised to God. Duties are our's; events are God's. Hannah knew this. What she promised she now performed. Her
prayer had been no light thing and not easily or casually
offered. Her's was a costly prayer and offered with tears
and strong crying. Time alone was not the least of the
cost. Strength of soul cried out for God so that she was
seen as drunk with sorrow.
(1) *She called the child Samuel.* Names were important
to the Israelite. Intrinsic lay the prophecy of life and the
name carried a meaning related to character. Why this
name for this boy? Because he was "asked of the Lord."
The name of Samuel means "name of God" or "heard of
God." How true that Samuel was *asked from God.* Her
vow was no bribe as though she pressured God on this
condition. She vowed out of devotion to indicate what
length she was willing to go in sacrifice for this child.
Samuel was *given by God.* As a baby he came as all others

by nature, yet his coming was not in God's providence when husband and wife sought to be parents. God had his time and place for that child. Samuel was trained and molded by his mother more than by his father. In a special way and to an unusual degree we trace her influence on Samuel. As a God-given child his destiny had been determined beforehand.

(2) *She devoted herself to him.* No mother gave stricter attention to her babe than Hannah. How precious was this child born late in married life. She nursed him as a child and when the time came for him to be weaned she knew what to do with him thereafter. His place had been pre-determined by God and in her heart. Hebrew mothers weaned their children later than moderns. After a number of years this was done. During those waiting years Hannah gave herself to her son. How precious those years are for all mothers. They are the creative and formative years. The child receives the first impressions of home and love, of God and duty. A mother can do more for history than anyone else. The early teaching is also a foundation for character and knowledge.

(3) *She dedicated her child to God.* Her husband went periodically to God's house for worship and to keep his vows. Hannah deferred until the young Samuel was ready to be given back to God. She now offered the sacrifice of thanksgiving and dedication. The feast or celebration brought much joy to her and her husband. She knew that she had trained her boy for the service of God and of God's house. She brought Samuel to hand him over in this act which carried out her solemn obligation and vow made years before. When she came before Eli she reminded him that she was the woman he had misjudged in the temple when she prayed with a sorrowful spirit. But now she

came to remind Eli that the promised child was ready to be dedicated to God. "For this child I prayed; and Jehovah hath given me my petition which I asked of him: therefore also I have *lent* him to Jehovah; as long as he lives he is lent to Jehovah." The word implied that he was *granted* or given back. For Hannah to lend Samuel would imply she could take him back again. No such thought was implied, but the reverse. She now gave him to God forever. In that hour and on "he [Samuel] worshipped Jehovah there." As a lad and later as a man he gave his life to the highest of all tasks.

V. The Sacrificial Heart, 2:1-11

Behind this story of Hannah is the spirit of willing obedience and ready sacrifice on her part. She was a woman who had no reservations in her faith toward God. Others have had this spirit. Mary of Nazareth and of Bethlehem in becoming the Mother of our Lord knew the same heart-pangs of Hannah. She, too, sang a prayer-hymn and *Magnificat* in presenting her child to God. Think of Susannah Wesley and her large family of nineteen with her illustrious sons: John the preacher, Charles the hymn-writer, and Samuel the hospital builder. What about Catherine Booth the mother of the Salvation Army and her large family sent out into the world to serve only God. How many mothers known to us have stamped their influence upon us through the faith they had in God and his purpose for us? Many of us have been dedicated before we were born, and lived to see mother's prayers fulfilled. The sacrificial heart is also the singing heart as this prayer-song indicates.

(1) *Hannah's song.* She continues in prayer at the dedication of her son. Samuel has been presented to the Lord.

Eli the High Priest has accepted him and he is now en-
rolled in the sanctuary school for further training and
service. His duties will be simple at first but increase in
responsibility. The climax will come when he is made the
prophet of God over Israel. Such was the destiny of the
young child Samuel. He was the child of promise, asked
for and given by God. Nothing unselfish is here in her
prayer for her son. Her joy is manifest in song. The theme
is a Magnificat as Mary's later is based upon it (Luke 1).
Within its praise are two emphases—that God is holy and
God is a God of knowledge. Here is the secret of the faith
of Hannah—she worshipped before God who had revealed
himself in this way. She could ask for this child knowing
that in returning him she would see him holy—separated
unto God. As God was full of knowledge so she prayed
that her son would have knowledge—for his service and
ministry. These things came to pass and her cup of thanksgiving was full.

(2) *Hannah's satisfaction complete.* In the days ahead
for Samuel she envisaged him growing in strength and
serving God acceptably. This is the noble ambition of
true motherhood. Her family life was blessed with more
children (vv. 20, 21). She made him a robe each year as he
grew so that he had a distinctive garb for his service. She
also continued the yearly sacrifice and offering to God in
worship as she came to God's house. Her reward lay in
the knowledge that, as she was in touch with the House of
God, she could see her son busy at his tasks and carrying
out his duties under the training of Eli. "Samuel ministered before Jehovah, being a child" (v. 18). Young as he
was he was one of the servants of God. A mother's heart
will never be fathomed in its joy or sorrow. What greater
afterglow of life is there than the knowledge that she has

worked with God in giving a son to the world for the service of God? Whatever Samuel did—helping Eli; candle-lighting; running errands; holding a dish; opening a door; or assisting at the altar—these were but the prelude to the greater work of the prophet to follow.

In all this is the devotion of Hannah. She kept her promise by keeping faith with God. Her's was the loving heart and the humble spirit.

7

Jonathan,
Noble in Friendship

Friendship is one of the most valuable traits in human life. When given by one person to another there is a grace bestowed and a glory given. He who has a friend is rich, and he who has more than one is in danger of being spoiled. How true this is can never be adequately measured. It was Ralph Waldo Emerson who said, "A friend is one in whose presence you can think aloud." By that standard we have few of the inner circle. The great literature of the ages has many stories of friendship. Acquaintances are many but friends are few. The true friend is one who would give his life for the other. Time and distance do not alter true friendship. Nothing changes the loyalty of one heart to the other. That God gives his friendship to men is taken for granted as we speak of the divine love in its out-going and grace. Among the outstanding stories of friendship is that of David and Jonathan.

I. Jonathan's Loyalty to Home and Friends. I Samuel 13, 14

The character of Jonathan stands out in a day of moral declension. The times of the Judges had passed and Israel had their wish granted to have a king like other nations. The nation was still in a time of organization and settlement. Saul became the first king and his eldest son is Jonathan, heir-apparent. The clear picture of Jonathan emerges gradually in the record.

(1) *Loyal to his father.* He fights the battles of the king and as a soldier has been trained in war. Almost single-handed Jonathan proves his skill and strength when he attacks the Philistines. Mistakes are sometimes made in the heat of battle. One such was in the result of Saul's command that those fighting should not partake of the spoil and not eat on one occasion. This was an oath. Jonathan evidently did not know of this and when he took honey and was strengthened he caused the others to follow his example in taking the spoil. When this was reported to Saul, he was angry and demanded the arrest of any found guilty, even to his son. However, the people rescued Jonathan and all was well. This was something which caused tension between the son and his father and became greater as David entered the picture. Jonathan however continued loyal to his father and served him.

(2) *Loyal to his friend.* When Jonathan first saw David we do not know. Perhaps it was the time when David slew Goliath. We can imagine how the young prince was thrilled at this exploit. His soul would go out in appreciation for the younger man's deed and achievement. This is the first recorded occasion when they met. David was brought before Saul to be thanked for his services. He was an unknown stripling, a mere youth, a champion unexpected. We can picture this scene as David is shown honor and respect for what he had done. Standing by the

king is Jonathan, and this is the moment when there are the stirrings of a first seal of that friendship which will endure through every test and trial for the rest of their lives (cf. 18:1).

II. Jonathan's Covenant with David, I Samuel 18

A covenant was a bond between two parties. In this enactment there was a pledge of devotion one to another. Whether this was for business, for a marriage plan, or for the uniting of families, the same principle was there. These two men were brought together into a bond of friendship.

(1) *"The soul of Jonathan was knit with the soul of David."* How mysterious are the ways of providence. How is it that two strangers meet and something passes between them which binds them as one? It is inscrutable how the unknown become known to each other, how life blends with life in love. Jonathan's heart went out to David. With warmth and beauty the story is told of the joining of these two men in affection and understanding. Age has nothing to do with it. It is true they were fighters and Jonathan the elder was impressed with the prowess of young David in the fight with Goliath, but this was but the beginning of the life-long friendship. The language is expressive. "Knit"—you knit things together that are of the same substance. Fiber, texture, strength, and endurance are words used of things which are woven as one by weavers in cloth. Threads and cords are intertwined to give strength and beauty of appeal. The Scripture suggests that the inner life of Jonathan was one of pristine beauty and that David also was a young man of moral strength. Up to that time each had lived aloof from others in the knowledge that they had not met anyone to complement their mental and spiritual powers.

(2) *"Then Jonathan and David made a covenant. . . ."*
This was inevitable. How else could an unknown stripling
like David have anything to do with the king's son? He
could not overture his new found friend as rank and position made that impossible. But Jonathan could himself
initiate this new relationship and did. The lowly shepherd
boy and the heir to the throne become fast friends. Socially
and in other ways there was nothing to make this come
to pass. The wonder is that there is nothing like it in all
the stories of friendship apart from God's love in Christ
for us. Another difficulty lies in the fact that Saul, Jonathan's father, does not like David and shows his hatred for
him. In spite of this, Jonathan has no reservations in his
friendship for David. This transcends the difficulties and
barriers. Many are the stories of love of a man for a
woman and these have been enshrined in song and poetry,
but nothing compares to this story of two men finding
their common bond in friendship which is bound in a
covenant relationship.

The signs and seals of this covenant are expressed in
that "Jonathan stripped himself of the robe that was upon
him, and gave it to David, and his apparel, even to his
sword, and to his bow, and to his girdle." This divestiture
was a deed of devotion unparalleled. The covenant required a seal and sign. The rainbow was the sign of the
covenant with Noah. Baptism in water and the Lord's
Supper in bread and wine remind us of signs and seals in
those ordinances and sacraments of the Christian church.
In marriage a ring is given and often another exchanged.
But in Jonathan's act is the gesture to share with David
his kingdom to be! He was the heir to the throne and
therefore the prince waiting to become king. This was
his destiny marked out for him by birth and position. Yet

here he would strip himself of his outward garb to seal his friendship with David and pledge that all he would have would also be David's. How selfless is Jonathan! How noble a gesture he makes. David was now given a place at court and had the dress of royalty to move in and out with freedom. Saul accepted him at first because of Jonathan and David was given a position of leadership over the soldiers and in the sight of the people.

III. Jonathan's Kindness to David, I Samuel 19

Following the new status afforded David, events led to the jealousy of Saul and David's life was endangered.

(1) *"Saul was wroth. . . .Saul eyed David. . . .Saul had his spear. . . .Saul was afraid of David. . . .Saul stood in awe of him. . . .Saul thought to make David fall. . . .Saul was David's enemy continually. . .*(cf. chap. 18). This is the background for the contrast of the attitude shown by Jonathan in comparison to that of his father Saul. Saul throughout is jealous of young David. As king he is recognized and praised for his deeds in war but the people make much more of David's acts. Envy can unmask a person. Hatred can be fanned by little things until the focus of a life is twisted. Saul becomes blind to any good in David and tried to get rid of him. He now saw him as a rival and did all in his power to put David out of the way. He schemed and plotted so that David might fall in battle but all in vain. And this, after he had lost control of himself in throwing a spear at David! Instead of accepting David as Jonathan's close friend and as a helper of Israel (cf. the defeat of Goliath), Saul despised the young man more than ever. Saul is a poor, pathetic figure at the last. He began under fair auspices in the morning of his life. He knew the glory of prosperity at high noon and should

have gone through the long day of his reign with honor. Instead he ended his life with a warped mind, with madness in his soul, and as a suicide at the last. To say that Saul was mad is the kindest way out, but it is also true that the Spirit of God had deserted him to his self-will and evil intent.

(2) *"Jonathan, Saul's son, delighted much in David."* In this opening verse of Chapter 19 lies the contrast of all that has gone before in Chapter 18. Jonathan had no illusions about his father. He warned David and assisted him to find a place of shelter and a way of escape from the jealous acts of Saul. He even offered to intercede with Saul on David's behalf in the hope that this might mitigate the evil designs against him. Jonathan reminds his father of David's bravery and faith in which he risked his life on behalf of the king and the nation. Who else stood up against the giant? Who else won victory over the Philistines? There came a period of quiet as Saul promised not to kill David. He was persuaded by Jonathan not to kill innocent blood. All went well for a while and then again Saul attempted murder by throwing a javelin at David. David escaped with the aid of his wife. Jonathan in all this is the one who stood by David. His friendship was under strain and test. He was the king's son and owed something to his father. But in this gesture of friendship for David he demonstrated that there can be a loyalty which transcends human kinship and blood in something greater. His kindness for David brought protection from death. The intrigue of a court, the upheaval of war, and the selfish ambition of a king brought danger to David so that he finally fled and left his friend Jonathan. In exile David has much to learn and receives a discipline of soul

for other days to come. Jonathan goes against his father Saul and stands by David.

IV. Jonathan's Devotion to David, I Samuel 20—23

The risks ran by Jonathan are obvious when he again and again stands by David and escapes the anger and threats of a jealous man, Saul.

(1) *A renewed covenant* (cf. 20). David's flight from Saul meant exile and loneliness. He had few to be with him and the outlook was dark indeed. Here Jonathan reveals those traits which mark him off as a man of principle and a man of his word. He never fails David. His coming to David is most touching and his reassurance to him most heartening. David is aware that Saul does not like his friendship with Jonathan and therefore pleads with Jonathan to be careful. The story that unfolds in this chapter is full of the thrill of a tale which has its plot and counter-plot. Reading it slowly and imaginatively is to find how Jonathan plans to save his friend. The visit home and the meals; the reaction of Saul to the absence of David; the renewed threats to kill David; then Jonathan's plea for David which brings Saul's hatred upon him. Finally, how Jonathan uses strategem to inform David that his life is in danger and that now he must leave for safety. At the heart of this chapter is the action where the covenant is renewed. This is no new covenant—rather the confirmation of the earlier one (vv. 12-16). Jonathan knew that the future held little for him as a possible king and that when his father was dead changes would come. He, therefore, wished to have the assurance from David that whatever happened David would never forget him and would be kind to him and to his family. "So Jonathan made a covenant with the house of David. . ." (v. 16). "And Jonathan caused David

to swear again, by his love toward him; for he loved him as he loved his own soul" (v. 17).

(2) *A remarkable devotion* (cf. chap. 23). In between Chapters 20 and 23 is the record of David's days of exile when he was hunted and harried by his enemies. One time he feigned madness to escape death. At the cave of Adullum he gathers more men who share his lot and who will one day help to place him on the throne. He is now an outcast and a rebel in the eyes of Saul. Saul continues to seek him and pursue him. The time is running out and it is expected that Saul will yet find him and kill him. It is here that Jonathan at the risk of his life seeks out David and shows his friendship and devotion once more. David has a few friends and fellow-soldiers to fight with him. The odds are against him. The one friend upon whom he can depend arrives—Jonathan. His life is also in danger but he risks everything to show he stands by David. Another covenant is entered into—another ratification of the earlier ones. At the heart of this is that thrilling declaration—"he strengthened his hand in God" (v. 16). At the time he needed encouragement it came! To strengthen his friend was to encourage him to have faith in God. Physically and materially David had little with which to fight Saul. He was no match for an army. But in the vale of soulmaking his life had a reinforcement of moral and spiritual power. Without this David could not have continued. The friendship of Jonathan brought this to him in the day of the ordeal. Misfortune is a testing time for friendship. Jonathan brought to David courage and faith to go on. At the same time he pledged to David his life as a servant as well as his friend. Jonathan does not ask David to help him to become king; he lays down his kingly prerogatives to bring David his sword.

V. Jonathan's Monument and Eulogy, II Samuel 1 and 9

After the hunted years and the days of exile, David returned good for evil in sparing Saul's life when he could have killed him. Saul died finally as a suicide and Jonathan died with him. David becomes king instead of Jonathan. His friendship continues unabated. Change does not cause it to wither and decay.

(1) *The Lament over Saul and Jonathan* (1:17-27). In all the noble tributes ever given to the departed this is outstanding. In this tribute of love and affection lies David's respect for his enemy Saul and his love for his friend Jonathan. "Lovely and pleasant in their lives." How true in reflection to see the retrospect which can omit the faults and see only the good qualities. The gracious acts of Jonathan reflected his inner serenity of spirit. He was a man who was good and true. There was a nobility of character which never stooped to the cheap and tawrdy. In contrast to the churlishness of others Jonathan could do no mean thing. By nature we might expect Jonathan to inherit some of the bad traits of his father Saul. Nothing of this is seen. The grace of God works in nature and heredity! He is like the knight of medieval days whose promise is only his word and whose actions will never sully or stain his shield. His chivalry is marked and his devotion is unstained. "Swifter than eagles, stronger than lions" tells of David's estimate of his friend who came to him at any hour of need—this was the heart of the covenant of friendship.

(2) *The Love that was wonderful* (v. 26). "Very pleasant hast thou been unto me: Thy love to me was wonderful, passing the love of women." In this final emphasis David sums up his friendship with Jonathan. As we think especially of Jonathan we trace the sacrificial nature of his

devotion and loyalty. Human life has nothing more wonderful and transforming than the love of a good and pure woman for a man. What higher tribute could be made of Jonathan's friendship than this? Going back to those early days we recall how Jonathan was ready to "speak good of David" (I Sam. 18:4), a touch of friendship always acceptable. When we need a friend how much this means! There was also the time when he took David to Saul and "Showed him all those things, and he was in his presence as in times past" (I Sam. 18:7). What a record of consistency and constancy. Jonathan ever sought the best for his friend. He told him all that had happened for good or ill. That is a true friend who tells you the truth, whether it hurts or not. Jonathan stood by his friend in sunshine and in shadow. That love endured to another generation. In II Samuel 9 is the story of how David remembered his covenant and friendship "fear not—Mephibosheth—for I will surely show thee kindness *for thy father's sake*." Thus does friendship send out into life living streams of blessing to others.

We may not end this picture of Jonathan as a friend without seeing something of another picture portrayed later in the New Testament. The parallel is there. Jesus Christ is a Son and He comes to show his friendship with the nobodies. He strips himself of the insignia of royalty in coming and when he takes us into his circle of friends he gives us what we lack and gives as a status of royalty. All this came from the fact that he loved first of all, and we, too, can say, "Thy love to me was wonderful." Christ also made a covenant with his people and pledged himself to us for ever. He stands by in our struggle and he is there always from one generation to another in devotion and love. Jonathan's love for David had in it something of the love of God which transcended human love as they had known. This surpassing love is the choicest gift of life—"ye are my friends." Friendship cannot be earned or bought—it is always given.

Amos,
Crusader for Righteousness

When God has a work to do He raises up a man who is willing to be wholly dedicated to His will. Such a man was Amos in the period of Israel's history (B.C. eighth century). The prophets of the Old Testament are seen to have been men of vision. They testify that God has come to them in moments of crisis and moments of ecstacy. Vision had in it heightened imagination and they told of "seeing" what others could not see. They were known as seers as well as prophets because of the insights they reported. This came by way of preaching and exhortation and sometimes by writing. They spoke with an authority unknown today. But vision was not given solely for the enjoyment of the prophet. He soon found that he had a task to perform, a need to be met. Amos, for example, was confronted by a situation in the Northern Kingdom (cf. Ten Tribes—Israel) that called for a strong and clear voice. The cessation of hostile attacks had brought prosperity to the land, but with prosperity came decadence. The temples were thronged, but religion had no connection with morality.

The priests seemed to vie with one another in making their shrines attractive, but with dubious attractions. Amid the extremes of riches and poverty Amos saw that justice had gone from the land. The weights were falsified and food adulterated. In this situation Amos knew himself to be called of God to fight this decadent society in the name of God's righteousness.

I. The Crusader, 1:1, 2

He left his simple occupation as a shepherd and a herdsman to engage in a difficult task. What kind of man was he? He came from the hill-country and looking after flocks. He was no product of the schools and lacked any higher levels of education. He was not like the priests of Bethel with all their advantages. His schooling was the open air, the wild beasts he fought, the crops he garnered, the flocks he nurtured, and the starry heavens at night. In the solitude of the distant hills of Palestine he kept communion with God.

The date is marked as "the time before the earthquake." All Israel would recall that event and so would know the coming of Amos as prophet. He was to proclaim righteousness and thunder the justice of God to the nation. From the hill country Amos could see the caravans pass and watch the march of armies. When he visited the cities he saw the contrast of life with his own. He sensed the seriousness of sin and the failure of society by its indulgences and selfishness. The fire of God burned within him and he could not be silent. "The words of Amos" marks the beginning of a new era. Israel's history and the world's religious life would not be the same again. The prophets mentioned in the earlier books of the Old Testament served their nation well, but time and again the people drifted into idolatry. Amos came to crusade against sin by denouncing injustice and calling for repentance. His message was preserved and later written down.

The fringe of the desert and the simple life of the nomad was not unknown to Amos. Valleys and hills intertwined for the making of obstacles to his work among his flocks with the danger of wild beasts and the threat of robbers. Amos 7:14, 15 tells how he makes no claim to greatness. He is a lowly person in Israel. He has no background of tradition or heritage to commend himself, "I was no prophet, neither was I a prophet's son. . . ." He was essentially "a man of the people." The little town of Tekoa, twelve miles south of Jerusalem, was his home and he had not far to go to visit the city with its life of ease and idolatry. To see Amos and then to hear him thunder forth the message entrusted to him would be an unforgettable event. "The Lord roars from Zion. . ." is no word of easygoing religion but a clarion call for action to follow. The land knew thunder, earthquake, and hurricane and in these terms Amos echoes the blast of the storm—not in nature but one coming upon a nation facing the judgments of God.

II. The Indictment, 6:1-7

Amos comes upon the people of his day with the voice of judgment. The corruption and impending doom which was there stabbed his conscience and forced him to speak out in boldness and power.

(1) *Judgment against Israel.* In 3:1-15 is the background which impels this indictment. Amos speaks of the nation as the family which God brought up out of Egypt. "You only have I known of all the families of the earth: therefore will I visit upon you all your iniquities." The nation

would expect Amos to thunder against her enemies, but they are startled that he speaks against them. The fact that they are God's elect people made them think they were safe and secure. Because they were the chosen people Amos said they would be judged. Privilege brings responsibility. This word of Amos has been described as *one of the turning points in the history of spiritual religion.* In this word "therefore" lies the stress which points out the accountability of all for their deeds. To whom much is given of the same shall much be required. Israel prided herself upon being the chosen nation in covenant relation with God. Now Amos would remind her that her call was a call for duty and service. There was nothing of favoritism in that choice. She was chosen to hold up before the world the example of a higher life under God.

In his trenchant utterance Amos colorfully describes the life of his day as illustrating what happens in the nation when judgment falls. He speaks of those who do violence and robbery in high places; of the pitfalls awaiting them when the enemy comes to plunder. There he uses illustrations from his shepherd-life; how he has rescued a leg or piece of an ear of one of the flock out of the lion's mouth. If Israel is rescued it will not be without some tragic happening and suffering. He foretells the destruction of the altars of Bethel and the palatial houses of the well-to-do with their attendant luxuries.

(2) *Moral breakdown described.* In 4:1-6 Amos vividly portrays how the women of the land have fallen down in morality. The "kine" refers to the female sex. Their days are spent in crushing the poor and the needy, and at the same time indulging in strong drink. The ivory couches are there, the splendor of the feasts, the ravishing music, the cosmetics used, and the drunken revelry. All this is

associated with an utter disregard for the affliction of the nation. The sins of gluttony, intemperance, and insolence are reprimanded by the prophet. On the eve of the French Revolution, the society of that nation was indifferent to the privations and poverty of the poor while at the same time they indulged in every form of luxurious debauchery. Dogs were better fed than children and the wine flowed red before the streets eventually ran red with blood. Israel was in a similar state. The sinful were warned of impending doom as in a time when a plague strikes but no one heeded. Sad indeed is the nation when the women lower their standards for then the slide is accelerated in delinquincy and moral turpitude.

(3) *Religious hypocrisy exposed.* In 5:18-21 satire is used by the prophet to unmask the people. They claim to be very religious. Alright, says Amos, then you ask for the day of the Lord to come when everything will be prosperous for all. But, says Amos, the reverse will be true for Israel. It will be darkness for light. Fleeing from a lion a sheep meets a bear and there is no escape—so the nation attempts an escape from responsibility to meet a greater judgment. Religious feasts and solemn assemblies are no substitute for moral honesty and justice. Even worship with its praise and giving cannot take the place of the humble heart and the repentant sinner. Hypocrisy is no offering for holiness of life. There needed to be a return to the Lord Jehovah and a renewal of moral life. The nation was urged to seek God again and to put away injustice, the sin which tore at the vitals of the people. Popular religion was exposed for what it was—a travesty of spiritual worship. Ceremony was not a substitute for consecration. Sacrifices had no validity when the moral life of the offerer was lacking in devotion and goodness. They wished for the

Day of the Lord to come and vanquish their enemies and give them special privileges. Amos painted a grim picture of that day when God would catch up with them in judgment and moral indignation.

The indictment is realistic and in depth. The words of Amos in 6:1-7 find the nation guilty on several counts. There is no escape for Israel. The pride of the people, their distorted sense of values, and their fear of disaster which could overtake them is most marked. The upper classes of Samaria are foolish as they swagger in their boastfulness. Are not they the first of all people? Their prosperity in material things gives them a false security. They become soft and an easy prey to the enemy. They had become the decadent society—not unlike much that is common today. Living at ease in Zion has made them to sin against God. Ease leads to evil. A nation which flaunts its luxury and licentiousness in the face of the under-privileged and oppressed, is a nation on the skids of disaster and under the sentence of death. The tragedy of it all is the blindness which cannot see the truth of the situation as depicted by the prophet. The fall of Rome had similar traits when the soft decadent life was their undoing. When discipline goes and moral standards are flouted a nation is in danger of losing its soul. The revellers have their way in society and blind leaders lead the nation to destruction.

III. The Plumb Line, 7:10-13

One of the startling figures of speech used by the prophet is this. The conscience is probed and the mind is searched as with a searchlight. In the imagery of the plumb line God lays bare the emptiness and the hollowness of the inner life of Israel.

(1) *Here is testing and examination.* How vivid is this word from Amos. The plumb line is used to test a building whether it has been built true or not. In the judgment of the prophet the house of Israel was not straight and plumb. The wall was tilted somewhat. It must fall eventually. There will come a crash. Doom has been predicted and a tragic destiny is foreseen. Given in a number of visions seen by the prophet each one unfolds little by little the inevitable end of the nation. There is *the vision of locusts* with the sequence of plague and disaster. *The vision of the onrushing fire* which consumed everything in its path followed. Next came *the vision of the wall and the plumb line.* At this point there is an intervention when Amos the prophet clashes with Amaziah the priest. Again there is given *the vision of the basket of summer fruit* suggesting the decay and the end of the nation's existence and life. *The final vision is that of seeing God himself* whose voice thunders "I will smite" (9:1).

Looking back to these earlier visions we find that the prophet foretells the disaster to the nation in terms of *locusts, fire,* and *plague.*

Only the intercession of Amos warded off the blow at that time. Amaziah the priest attempted to destroy the witness of Amos (7:10-13) in smearing him before the people with lying words. He tried to discredit what Amos said and then tried himself to speak smooth and lying things to the people. He also threatened Amos that he should not preach anymore as Bethel was the king's sanctuary and a royal house. Not that this intimidated Amos. He could withstand the wiles of a false prophet in the guise of a priest.

(2) *Here is tragedy and trouble* (8:4-12). As Amos had foretold, Israel suffered grievously at the hands of her

enemies and under the judgment of God. Captivity and exile were part of the nemesis of judgment. Persecution and trial were commonplace experiences of the nation in after years. They became a scattered people. The plumb line with its metal bob or plummet at the end touches the vertical direction of the wall being tested. Israel was judged accordingly by God. The nation measured itself horizontally as men do comparing one with another, but God judges vertically—man in comparison to God's commandments. The warning was repeated by Amos and the nation was without excuse. The text here speaks of the sins of injustice in sharp business practices, the eagerness to have done with the Sabbath rest in order to make more money on the following day, the robbery of people and the deceits practiced in trade, the enslavement of individuals who are bound by a price.

God speaks here of judgment, of a night coming in its darkness and gloom from which there is no relief. They might well fear this long night when no sunshine would attend their way. It would be as a day of mourning for one dead, even an only son, and "the end thereof as a bitter day." Because they had violated the Sabbath Day they were to know in retribution the day of darkness. They had complained about the Sabbath Day and wished for other days to make money and profits! It was boring to sit out a Sabbath when they might have been making money, so they had reasoned. The final eclipse for them lay in the tragic fact of a time when there would be "a famine for the word of Jehovah." Nothing could be worse than that! As long as the word of God is available there is hope of recoverability. Amos had said earlier—"seek God" and now when they had not sought him they were faced with a spiritual famine. America faces a situation in which in our day there are forces at work removing the Bible from the public schools so that God is not acknowledged as before in that way of reading the book. This by a nation "under God." How close we are to Israel in the days of Amos.

(3) *Here is healing and hope* (9:11-15). Although the judgments of God were certain and sure, Amos had a word of mercy in the midst of that stern note. His chief emphasis in preaching lay in *the Righteousness of God revealed*. Israel might boast of her election and take pride that she was the chosen people, but this was no escape from moral rightness and spiritual rectitude. Amos was a reformer and a prophet whose task was to summon the nation back to God and to the standards of righteousness. He thundered forth the judgments of God which were inevitable, but he also spoke a word of healing and hope. This lay in the promise of another day of the Lord wherein righteousness would reign. This was to be a day of restoration and renewal, of return and recompense. The absolute righteousness of God is a theme ever present for Israel and all nations. Judgment is inevitable and there are no exceptions. The privileged people have greater responsibility. The religion which was form and ceremony and lacked moral living was under sentence of judgment. The injustices of life in a society were also under scrutiny. If a nation is to examine itself then it must do so by the divine standards and not by any comparison with other nations and their practices. All privilege is to be held in trust for God and for others. A nation cannot live to itself just as an individual dare not in the light of the Ten Commandments and especially in the light of the teaching of our Lord.

This then was Amos—the champion for God who fought vested interests, entrenched evil, and lowered moral standards. Bad religion as well as corrupt business practices knew his scathing denunciation. The sordid wanton ways of the rich who cared not for their fellow-men were held up to ridicule and scorn. The corruption of society at all levels knew his rapier thrust of irony and satire in judgment. Amos was not an "ordained" priest like the priests of Bethel. He lacked their schooling. He had no earthly right to be called a prophet. But God called him and gave him his ministry. It was unorthodox and yet effective in appeal. A nation stopped and listened. They did not hear comfortable words. They were not flattered or pleased. The fire of judgment came upon them through this prophet.

If Amos came to town what would happen? Would he stand in Times Square, New York or at Hyde Park corner, London? Would he pass by our churches and institutions and visit the city hall and our leaders of capital and labor? Of course he would come to our churches for therein lies the place where people worship before they take their lives into the market places of the world during the week. Would Amos speak to us today as he spoke to Israel long ago? We know the answer. He would criticize our institutions and search out our motives in worship and work, in politics and social customs. His word would be like a plumb line once more and we would know it. Our drinking habits, our immoralities, our sharp practices in business, our feather-bedding, our cheating and lying, our sins would all come under his lash. He would whip us to bring us to healing. He would stab our conscience to bring us to a mighty hope in God's salvation. A prophet like Amos who tells us the truth is our true friend as he crusades for righteousness.

Josiah,
Statesman-Reformer

The story of young Josiah is one that stands out in the Old Testament in a time when Israel needed men of high character and leadership. In the listing of the kings it is well to remember that the Northern Kingdom had nineteen kings in all and the Southern Kingdom had nineteen kings and one queen. Of these the record fluctuates between good and bad. Only four could be said to be good in Judah and among these was Josiah. Before him was Manasseh his grandfather and for fifty-five years the nation was like a moral desert in its barrenness and unfruitfulness. Declension into sin and flagrant evil were commonplace. When Josiah succeeded his father Amon to the throne he was but a youth, a minor, under regency and already subjected to the foul atmosphere of a bad court.

I. His Reign, II Kings 22:1; II Chronicles 34

When he was eight years of age his father Amon died and Josiah reigned thirty-one years in Jerusalem over Judah. Manasseh had been murdered and his going was no loss in the moral climate of that day. His influence had been pernicious and unwholesome. Manasseh's son Amon reigned only two years (cf. II Kings 21:19) and his record was also stained with evil deeds. Innocent blood was shed freely and idolatry was an accepted way of life.

(1) *Influences on his life.* Although the inheritance of Manasseh and Amon was bad Josiah was young enough not to have been swayed too much by their wicked example. A child sees and hears more than can be understood at the time. Example guides a child into action for good or evil. The first eight years of life are the most impressionable years. Fortunately there was his mother Jedidah, or "Beloved." She was a good and noble woman who devoted herself to her son. She would instill into him those finer traits of moral conduct which alone a mother could with her unceasing vigilence and devotion to her charge. Her training in the traditions of the Hebrew people gave him a foundation for his later life. History tells of other mothers whose gracious ways trained noble men. Samuel owed much to Hannah; Augustine had Monica; the Wesley brothers had Susannah.

(2) *Inheritance given him.* The outward trappings of the kingdom were not bright but tawdry. The throne was not held in high regard after two evil kings. Religion had been stained with idolatry and the Temple was in a bad state of disrepair. Over all, lay the impending threat of judgment coming from stronger enemies without and certainly the knowledge that God could not overlook their evil ways as a nation. Although Manasseh and Amon had left him nothing but trouble, there was the remembrance of his great ancestor king David. His name and influence was still known to the people and obviously to young Josiah. Heritage is worthwhile when we think of what it

can do to turn the tide for good. Others in the nation comprised the small group of faithful, believing Hebrews known as the Remnant. They kept alive the spirit of true worship and devotion to God. Some of them are named in this chapter in Hilkiah the high priest, Shaphan the scribe, Huldah the prophetess, and others. Amid the corruption at Court and a ruined Temple, Josiah had his spiritual advisers in these people who stood for righteousness.

II. His Regeneration, II Kings 22:2-3a; II Chronicles 34:1-3

"He did that which was right in the sight of the Lord, and walked in the ways of David his father; and declined not neither to the right hand nor to the left. For in the eighth year of his reign, while he was yet young, he began to seek after the God of David, his father" (II Chron. 34:1-3). This was his conversion experience.

(1) *His decision was for the right person.* He sought God. Through his mother's influence and training he had a knowledge of God but it was second-hand. Now came his own act of faith at sixteen years of age. The Chronicler supplements the record of Kings in noting that Josiah was yet young when he came to this supreme decision. The major decisions of life are made in youth. Youth matured quickly in the East and Josiah was at the dawn of manhood and adulthood. By this time he would have passed his Bar Mitzvah and become a son of the congregation and assumed his adult state. He was ready then for this transforming hour. Here is the right beginning for Josiah.

(2) *His decision was at the right time.* Youth is the best time for a life to know the heart of God in love and committal. Then will come growth in moral stature and in spiritual understanding. A goodly heritage from his mother

and with helpful religious leaders standing by, Josiah knew the contrast from the evil example of his father and grandfather. Now he decides for himself. "While yet young" suggests the time was ripe. Conversion experiences find their height around this age. Many there are who may not be able to pin point an hour or a time (cf. young Timothy), but in Josiah's case there was a crossing over into newness of life in a decisive way. The period of youth with its play and irresponsibility recedes and the sphere of duty beckons. The entire outlook on life is changing. How much more at the place of devotion and worship!

(3) *His decision was in the right manner.* "He did right in the sight of the Lord." Here was an earnest spirit and sincerity of heart. He did not count the cost or think of the consequences. His choice was intelligent for he chose to live "in the ways of David." David's life was not free from stumbling and sinning, but as the shepherd-king who gave the Twenty-Third Psalm he exercised a life-long influence for good. The choice was also determined as he "turned not one way or another." Steadfastness of purpose is here. His resolution marked him off as a youth of strength and courage who would stand by his convictions.

III. His Reformation, II Kings 22:3b-7

Not everyone is called to such a high and exalted state to be a king. Most of us find humbler places and tasks. Josiah exemplifies the best for those who would follow God's ways and will. As a result of his conversion all parts of the nation's life felt his influence for righteousness.

(1) *At Home* (II Chron. 34:3b-7). He began to purge Judah and Jerusalem from the high places, the Asherim, the graven images, and the molten images. And he broke down the altars of the Baalim. This was the only way to

rid his people of idolatry. Reform begins at the House of God. He was now only twenty years of age when he began this task. At the Court as well as at the House of God men knew that a new man was in leadership. Changes were now inevitable. The corruption and pollution of idolatry was swept out.

(2) *In Jerusalem.* He burned the bones of the false priests upon their altars and cleansed Jerusalem (v. 5). What a story! If that were to be reported in modern fashion we can imagine the startling, bold headlines of a newspaper announcing this news item. The Temple needed cleansing and in his zeal Josiah overturned everything that hindered. It was not enough to get rid of the altars and customs of idolatrous worship; he also exterminated those who were the leaders of bad religion. Bones, relics, buildings, abuses, hypocrisies, shams, injustices, and all devilries were attacked and uprooted once and for all. The reformer may be iconoclastic but history speaks of men like Josiah who arise to get rid of the unclean and debasing. Martin Luther and John Knox later were not unlike Josiah. Evil does not deserve any quarter.

(3) *In Israel.* The nation and the whole land began to feel the stirring of a new day as Josiah worked his will. "Throughout the whole land" (vv. 6, 7) speaks of the comprehensive nature of this movement. Here was moral, social, and spiritual reform at its best. The city and the State knew that social and civic righteousness is not only demanded but is needed and will be introduced. We can never tell the full results of a life converted to God. Streams of good flow from that decision until vast areas of life are affected. Josiah's deeds are forever enshrined in the annals of the histories of Israel for all to read. He brought zeal and passion to his task. Although this work

is destructive it was necessary and a prelude to the second phase of reconstruction to follow.

IV. His Reconstruction, II Chronicles 34:8-13; II Kings 22:3-7

Disease and pestilence have to be stamped out before health can be enjoyed after a time of plague. So it was in Josiah's time. Now came the era of reconstruction which brought other problems to be solved. Josiah had the mind to see what was required and acted immediately.

All the bestial things, the drunkenness, the vice and immoralities, the sham religious practices, and the gross superstitious customs were swept away in the indignation and righteous wrath of Josiah. Youth is the best time for this spirit but it can be in evidence at any time of life when the time is ripe. There was a moral necessity for this to be done, but now Josiah had to tackle the more difficult job of rebuilding. Having plucked up the weeds in the garden he could attend to cultivating flowers. The ground was cleared and was ready for tillage and sowing.

The buildings of the Temple were first in his mind and plan. They had fallen into ruin and the sacred books of God were missing. His first act is to engage skilled men who would toil and work to renew what had been broken down. A collection of money was taken up so that the cost might be defrayed. This helped to pay wages as well as procure materials for the task. The money was more than sufficient in the generosity of the givers, and it was not necessary to reckon how much when the spiritual leaders could be trusted to use it aright. As the workmen began strange things happened.

V. His Revival, II Chronicles 34:14-28; II Kings 22:8-22; 23:1-30

As the workmen began they removed much rubbish from the ancient temple and its ruined condition. During this process Hilkiah the high priest was on hand and suddenly discovered a roll of parchments (cf. the excitement of finding the Dead Sea Scrolls) which proved to be the Temple copy of the Law. This was usually kept in the side of the Ark. Here was evidence of the low moral state and the spiritual declension of the nation when they had lost their sacred writings. Here was neglect and apostasy.

(1) *The discovery of the book* (II Kings 22:8). "I have found the book of the law in the house of Jehovah." In these words lies the beginning of a new day for Josiah and his people. Possibly lost for some sixty years, this word of God led the way back to renewal and revival of spiritual religion. Its existence must have been known and now with its return there must have been a sense of shame and guilt that those who were its custodians had ever lost it by their neglect. The scribe brought the book to Josiah and read from it before the king. The result was that the king rent his clothes, a sign that he was sorry and repentant. He had "a tender heart" and the light of truth easily stirred his conscience. The word of God had been lost in the place where it was supposed to be used. Its findings stabbed the conscience of the religious leaders. What to do next was questioned by Huldah, the prophetess, who did not think the people were ready for action. It was then that Josiah showed himself strong and heroic in being first to bring his life under the commands of the newly discovered book. When Martin Luther discovered the Bible in the Middle Ages he had the advantage of the whole Bible. Josiah had only a part, but it was sufficient.

(2) *The dedication of the people* (II Chron. 34:29-33). Urged on by Josiah, the leaders and the people brought themselves before the judgment and the searchlight of that word of God. The effect of its presence and the reading of it brought many to the place of repentance and renewal. "The king stood by the pillar, and made a covenant before the Lord, to walk after Jehovah" (II Kings 23:3). Josiah's example enabled him to enter into this Covenant relationship with God for himself and on behalf of the people. Whether the people as a whole followed sincerely is questioned, but a new day dawned for Judah by the king's action. He himself led in reading that word of God, so that the people knew by his action what was involved. He stood as the leader and head of the nation and what he did involved them also. There was a touch of creativeness and originality, a boldness in this. At the same time he cleansed the city of its anti-Jehovah elements in worship and life. He saw to it that due preparation was made for a renewed life of his people. He commanded them to obey the word of God and to follow Jehovah (II Chron. 34:33). The record indicates he was able to keep them to their promise so to do. Then came the Passover Feast (II Chron. 35:1-19), a time of rejoicing and gladness. The sacrifices were offered and the memorial kept. Not only had the Law of Moses been lost but they had neglected to keep the Passover, which was to be a perpetual memorial. By means of this service they renewed their vows and confessed they were God's Covenant people.

(3) *The delayed task of renewal.* Although Judah kept a Passover such as had not been known for many years, it was not enough. True, there was great enthusiasm and a splendid response to the demands of Josiah. Eight days

of festivity were enjoyed by all, but thereafter the people settled down again to accept what was given as routine. The glow departed and the zest went out of their religious life. A nation which had known evil leadership so long was not easily and quickly altered by young Josiah. He tried and succeeded, but partially. The decline in morals and the defection from true worship had seen the calamity come. After Josiah's death it became evident that he had only scratched the surface of what was deep seated. He had little support and yet he did an extraordinary act. At least outwardly the effects were manifest in his day. He saw his nation cleansed of the foul worship of evil gods and idols. He saw people hearing once again the word of God. He had the satisfaction of reinstating the Law of Moses and observing the Passover. In all these acts he was a witness to the fact that he had entered into a new life in relation to God and his life was dedicated to the will of God alone.

As a statesman and a reformer Josiah is given an honorable place in history. His work took place in one of the worst of times. His father and grandfather had been noted for their evil ways, and for some fifty-six years the people of Judah had known nothing but a bad example in leadership. Nations become like their leaders. Puritan England and Puritan New England were noted for certain ethical standards and religious ideals. These not only influenced that day but controlled most of the life of that time. When England in the eighteenth century had fallen into the blight of Deism and lax moral living it seemed that a fate similar to that of the French Revolution lay ahead. Mercifully God raised up John and Charles Wesley with their words and singing to stir the land until the people repented and found revival and

renewal of their moral life. The Evangelical Revival is
the watershed of our modern civilization with its Hebrew-
Christian standards and ideals. No revival touches everyone. There are always those who miss the blessing when
God visits a nation. It was so in Josiah's day. He is remembered for his leadership in revival and its results
changed the direction of the nation toward God.

When the final epitaph was written it said of Josiah
that "like unto him was there no king before him, that
turned to Jehovah with all his heart, and with all his
soul, and with all his might, according to all the law
of Moses; neither after him arose any like him" (II Kings
23:25). The words have a familiar ring for those of us
who know the language of the New Testament and the
word of our Lord Jesus Christ. He spoke of the first and
great Commandment. Moses had said "Thou shalt love
Jehovah thy God with all thy heart, and with all thy soul,
and with all thy might" (Deut. 6:5). This was part
of the Shema, the ultimate confession in God for the
Hebrew people. In the discovery of the Law, Josiah had
read these words and then gone on to live in their light
and strength. This was the secret of his moral power and
spiritual influence. To add (cf. N.T.) "With all thy mind"
is to see how true this was of Josiah. He gave intelligent,
bold, courageous, and original leadership in a dark hour
of history. All because his heart was tender to the Lord.

10

Baruch,
Faithful Secretary

We are surprised to light upon this man in tracing the story of Israel. In the work of the prophets we are impressed with the outstanding characters and then suddenly and almost incidentally a name is mentioned such as this one. What part does a man like this play in history? What has his life contributed that God has permitted a record of him in the Bible? Part of the surprise of Biblical history is the use God makes of obscure characters. They play a minor part and yet without them something would be missing. Thus it was with Baruch. *He was the link between the spoken word of God and the written word of God.* His life and work throw light upon one of the most crucial questions of our day—how were the Scriptures transmitted and what is involved in the revelation and inspiration of that word of God.

I. Reporting a Deed, Jeremiah 32:9-15
Our first glimpse of Baruch is to see him as the son of an unknown father and from a background of family

which does not have much importance for the recorder of Scripture. As Baruch had much to do with the recording of the words of Jeremiah, it may have been modesty on his part not to disclose any further information about himself. Controlled and inspired as he must have been for his work for God this could also be divine providence.

Baruch is the amanuensis of Jeremiah. In this he is the scribe or writer who carried out the reporting and recording of what is said. The existence of law led to a profession whose business was the study and knowledge of the law. From the days of Ezra certain priests and scholars gave themselves to this task. Gradually the scribes became a group apart from the religious leaders of the nation of Israel. There is no evidence that Baruch was a scribe in this professional sense, but rather one who did this work of copying and writing on behalf of others. He was an assistant and thus is termed a secretary. He was a close friend of Jeremiah (Jer. 32:12); the willing helper (Jer. 36:4, 32); and the faithful attendant of the prophet (Jer. 36:10-19; 45:5; 43:3, 6). Other writings have been attributed to Baruch—books of the Apocryphal type—e.g., *The Apocalypse of Baruch*—but these have no reference to this present task which was his with Jeremiah.

Jeremiah under the direction of God had bought a field in Anathoth. This land was about to pass into the hands of Babylon and the prophet himself was in prison. God ordained this transaction as a sign that one day God would restore the land to the people. Jeremiah although puzzled obeyed. Then Baruch was called and given the deed of purchase—"take these deeds, this deed of the purchase which is sealed, and this deed which is open, and put them in an earthen vessel; that they may continue many days." Baruch following the custom of the times becomes the surety for that deed of land. Our day would require registration of title and payment of a fee and the usual legal requirements endorsed. The depository for this deed was in an earthen vessel. Knowing now about the Dead Sea Scrolls and the custom of storing valuable scrolls in jars it could be that this was the method adopted by Baruch in his day. We know that in the East with its dry climate manuscripts or scrolls are preserved for a thousand years and more! Our first picture then of Baruch is that of a man carrying out his business in reporting the fact of what has taken place in the life of Jeremiah and preserving the deed for this particular transaction. Little did he think that the fact of it and the interpretation of it would be wrapped up in the history of Israel!

II. Recording the Word of God, Jeremiah 36:4

The Bible as we have it came slowly and in parts gradually as it was spoken and then recorded by hand. Part of the romance of its transmission lies in the many people —some unknown scribes and some known like Baruch— who shared in this providential task over hundreds of years. This humble and not well-known man was given the task under Jeremiah. The prophet requested him to "take down"—was this in shorthand of a kind or written out fully at the time?—his spoken word. In this sense Jeremiah dictated to a secretary. The prophet also preached and spoke in public under the inspiration and movement of God, and here Baruch would report the extemporaneous speech or produce a digest of what was said. Faithfully he recorded the spoken word.

Jeremiah claimed to have received "all the words of Jehovah which He had spoken unto him." This implied the fact of revelation from God, receiving from God that which could not be disclosed in any other way at that time. Under the guidance of the Holy Spirit we believe that Jeremiah was inspired or carried along in heightened imagination and thought to speak what God gave in thought and direction. The actual words of the prophecy can be found in Chapter 25 (several predictions) and especially in 36:2—"all the words that I have spoken to you against Israel and Judah and all the nations, from the day I spoke to you, from the days of Josiah until to-day." There is no suggestion here that God dictated the words to Jeremiah as they were given to him, but rather that Jeremiah dictated the words that the Lord had spoken to him previously to Baruch. As a prophet and preacher in proclamation he might have repeated some of these special themes so that after many years they would still be recalled to mind. The roll of the book referred to the scroll then in use by the Hebrews. The prophet was an inspired man who received God's words and then he gave by in-spiration those words to Baruch who also recorded them. The record then is found to be an inspired record and the word of God.

III. Reading the Sacred Scroll, Jeremiah 36:5-8

Instead of the prophet taking that recorded word of God and using it in the Temple he asks his secretary or scribe to do this. The prophet was more accustomed to rhapsodic speech in the open. The priest usually con-ducted the service of the house of God and interpreted the law, either by himself or the service of a scribe qual-ified in law. Jeremiah was restrained at this time and so Baruch read the word of God.

There is here the vital recognition that the scroll was

the divine word to be read and received without question. Jeremiah again repeats words which leave no other interpretation possible. "Read in the roll, which thou hast written from my mouth, the words of Jehovah in the ears of the people in Jehovah's house upon the fast-day" (v. 6). Here is the principle of God's work in producing the Scriptures. The inspired speaker has his words transcribed by a faithful secretary and that man—Baruch in this case—is also under the Spirit of God for his work so that he records only what is given—no more, no less. This written down word then is the word of God transmitted as a record of the revelation made by God in human life and now fixed in literature. The record before us is now the revelation of God and we receive by faith and obedience the illumination of the same Spirit who inspired Jeremiah and Baruch (vv. 17, 18).

Now we find Baruch reading the Scriptures to the people. No doubt he could give an emphasis and a stress as he read because of his feeling for that word and out of his familiarity with it. To him it was not new and unknown and so he became an interpreter of that word however simple his method. A similar scene comes later in the Sixteenth Century in England when the scarcity of Bibles led to one being chained in a parish church. There, by a pillar, people would gather around to listen to someone read. The result of Baruch's reading was the return of evil people back to God and his commands. Renewed prayer in supplications would follow as the result of hearing that word.

We are not told specifically that Baruch stood in a pulpit to read and it could be that he stood at the Gate of the Temple in the open air. Jeremiah was restrained by the hand of God and of course he was not popular either at the court of the king or in society. The message of judgment is never welcome. Baruch was courageous to take the prophet's place and read so that the word of God did its own work in the hearts of the hearers.

IV. Rejecting the Word of God, Jeremiah 36:22-26

One result of that reading of the Scriptures was manifested in the refusal of the king to accept the truth. Jehoiakim, the son of Josiah, the king of Judah, knew of this recital of God's word from the princes at his court who had heard Baruch. Evidently the scroll had been deposited with one of the Temple scribes (vv. 20, 21) and it was easy for the king to obtain it. He had it read and in his dislike and disdain he took a penknife and cut the pages in pieces and cast them into a fire. The faithful scribes pleaded with him but in vain. The king with his court were not afraid of the consequences and showed a spirit of opposition to that message they had heard. They utterly rejected the word of God. Truth was not welcome. God's voice was not heard by them. The word of God brought conviction and a sense of judgment upon the king but he would not accept this from God.

What happened then has been repeated in later days. The enemies of God have always fought against the Bible. Reports of the American Bible Society and the British and Foreign Bible Society tell of persecution wherever this word of God has gone. In the Middle Ages a dead and barren church in its apostasy fought the reading of the word of God. It was not given to the people. Copies of the Bible were destroyed. A Luther was opposed but he translated the Bible into his people's tongue and the Reformation was greater than ever. William

Tyndale of England was destroyed but his translation gave England a new birthright of freedom under the word of God. His translation became the foundation for that monument of English, the King James or Authorized Version, in 1611. The word of God has not been bound even though God's enemies have tried to destroy that word.

The action of the king that day in taking the scroll bit by bit and little by little to cut it up and burn it piece by piece is suggestive in its tragedy for him. Bible-burning has been a common practice ever since but strangely enough the Bible has increased in its circulation and influence throughout the world. The word of God is not destroyed by burning it—the truth it contains goes on unhindered. More modern days have seen the rise of enemies who have attempted to discredit the Bible by questioning its authority and veracity. Here again the word of God has not been destroyed. Whatever light is shed upon the Bible to set forth its truth from any quarter is to be welcomed. Discoveries in archaeology, the Dead Sea Scrolls, papyri studies, the fresh finds from antiquity and science—all these but bring us closer to the background of the times and customs of Bible lands and people. This leads to clearer knowledge of the words and idioms of speech and this in turn enables us to make more accurate translations for the thought and speech of our day. This is a never-ending task for the Christian church—to make clear and communicate the living, lasting word of God. Not the penknife but the pen is the instrument being used increasingly. Baruch knew that some rejected the word he read, but he also believed that what he did was not in vain.

V. Replacing the Lost Roll, Jeremiah 36:27-32

The actions of the king of Judah could easily have discouraged Jeremiah and Baruch in their work for God. Man acts in rebellion against God but God will over-rule for the good of all. Baruch and the prophet were in danger. Not only was the word of God rejected and consumed by the flames but their lives were threatened with death because of their association in writing that word. They were able to flee and find safety (v. 26). This was a providence of God and is so stated "God hid them."

"Take thee again another roll, and write in it all the former words that were in the first roll. . . ." In doing this Baruch was told to add the story of what the king had done and the prediction that the king of Babylon would come and invade the land of Judah. Here is the second writing of the word of God. What happens when a duplicate is made? The record is usually clearer than ever in the mind of the scribe. The content and data of the record are such that he will re-write with better understanding, and use language and idiom for all to understand. This second roll had all that was in the first and all its statements were carried out irrevocably. As this second roll had to be with "many similar words were added" (v. 32), so it must have been much longer than the first. Material in it had certain additions and certain omissions when we compare the actual text now before us. Here then is another stage in transcribing the word of God—a revision of material is made in selectivity, under divine guidance, by Baruch.

Enemies of God may attempt the destruction of the divine word but the word of God endures. God over-rules his enemies' actions and gives to the church more in the end. This principle has been carried out with other

portions of the Scriptures until we now have the entire
Bible as we know it. In the divine providence the pro-
phetical writings were recorded; the poetical books were
joined together; and then these were placed alongside of
the older writings of the law and the Torah. Thus the
canon of the Old Testament was completed and gradually
accepted by the Jews as the code for their life. The
Christian church inheriting these writings saw in them the
foreshadowing of much that was to come in Christ. "The
New was in the Old contained: the Old was in the New
explained." Not one without the other. The Christian
faith now rests upon both testaments. We owe much to
faithful Baruch who re-recorded and added other words
of the prophet to give us a more complete story of God's
ways with his people. Thus God preserves and propagates
his truth in all generations.

VI. Rewarding Faithful Service, Jeremiah 43 and 45

The summing up of Baruch's life and work is found
in fragments in this prophecy. Again this could be his
humble way of life and work. He would not intrude himself at any time. Only casually and incidentally do we
stumble upon his personal ways. God used this ordinary
man for great ends. Perhaps he did not realize the magni-
tude of what God was doing. He was, after all, a secretary
or scribe to a prophet. Periodically Jeremiah called him
aside to transcribe an oracle or report a speech. Sometimes he took the dictated words from the prophet. In all
this he made a contribution of far-reaching influence. He
was one of the men who helped to *write the Scriptures!*
Was there ever a more important task?

Chapter 43 tells of Baruch and Jeremiah going down
to Egypt for safety in a time of national crisis. They went

in fear of their enemies and these two men went grudgingly and unwillingly. Nevertheless they went as Baruch was under suspicion now (v. 3). The word he brought through writing as the word of the prophet was not liked and so he was blamed for catastrophe. The man who published the truth was not appreciated then as now. Judah's remnant in Egypt would not have long until Nebuchadnezzer's armies would sweep down again to engulf them.

Chapter 45 concludes the story of Baruch with but five verses as though he had written his signature on the scroll and leave the reader with a postscript after all. Again is the word of the Lord through Jeremiah to Baruch. As a close confidant of the prophet he shared these revelations and intimations of God. Having written parts here and there, it is not improbable that he finally put all together and thus gave us the text of Jeremiah the prophet. This is hinted at in Chapter 52 and 51:64—"thus far are the words of Jeremiah." This makes Chapter 45 significant. Baruch would seem to be swayed with the idea that he might be entitled to some appreciation for what he had done or was he dreaming of some reward? At any rate, God gave the final summing up by reminding him that true greatness lay in being himself and not seeking false ambition. God is the one who acts in and through his chosen instruments—Jeremiah was one and Baruch was another. Over against verse 5, "seekest thou great things for thyself? seek them not," could be placed a New Testament word—"seek ye first the kingdom of God." Baruch was in the forefront of that greater line who do God's will faithfully.

11

Ezekiel,
Pastor of His People

In the work of the ministry that of the pastor is held in high esteem. There are those today who would minimize its importance but, throughout Biblical times and during the history of the Christian church, this office was deemed to be vital for the welfare of people. Men might look to national leaders for direction in government and to educators for help in intellectual development, but the pastor has always been the one person to help people in their moral and spiritual needs. Before the modern trend to set up counsellors the pastor was that counsellor who would listen to his people in their homes or at the church. He expressed his care and concern for people in all walks of life. The pastor was a shepherd and one who led and fed the flock committed to his care. Among the prophets of the Old Testament emerges Ezekiel as one who stood in this gracious succession. His book reveals his heart of compassion for his people and his actions on their behalf. As a prophet we tend to see him as one proclaiming with passion and power. It is good to see this in the light of the fact that he was a pastor first of all and only as a pastor did he send out his call to the nation.

I. He Identified Himself with His Nation, 1:1-3

The vision given to him at the first told of this concern he had to be one with his people. "I was among the captives of Cheba:. . ." (v. 1). His nation had been led into captivity and it was easy for Ezekiel to be embittered and calloused as he brooded about their ills and disasters. Babylon was a mighty power, and the Judean kings, Jehoiakim and his son Jehoiachin, had found out that rebellion brought only total defeat and the destruction of their capital Jerusalem. Exile was never pleasant and hopelessness eroded away the spirit of those in captivity.

(1) *A pastor of hope.* This was the spirit which gripped the young spiritual leader. He refused to be defeated. In the darkest hours he still held on to the promises of God and affirmed that God would yet bring the nation through to its ultimate goal of restoration and renewal. Ezekiel was a realist in that he recognized the sins of his people and the rightness of their punishment under exile when they had rebelled against God. Chastisement was inevitable when the nation spurned the divine command-ments. Although Ezekiel is called a prophet and so exer-cised his ministry, he was also a priest of the Temple. However, his pastoral work emerges from those others and becomes the basic quality of his contribution to his people. The prophet can unveil evil and ask for judg-ment; the priest can pray and intercede for the penitent; but it is the pastor who must keep alive the spirit of hopeful endurance in the darkest hours of life.

(2) *A pastor of vision.* The record speaks of the visions of God granted to him in exile. The symbolism of the

wheels was a means by God to bring imagery and imagination to bear upon the solution of an almost insurmountable task. Only as one man as a pastor seeing this could God find a channel to communicate his message to the nation in its extremity. Behind the spirit of hope and assurance which Ezekiel had lay this mysterious experience of the vision. The days were dark and uncertain was the future—then came the wheels, the living ones, the fire, and the spirit of life (vv. 4-28). Visions were given to give direction and assurance in the midst of uncertainty and the spirit of defeatism then prevalent. God always comes to his servants through media close to their own personality and in this case a strong imagination can find symbolism effective.

(3) *A pastor of understanding.* Several times there is the allusion to the fact that "the hand of the Lord was there upon him" (v. 3). Linked with that is the testimony of Ezekiel "I heard a voice of one that spake" (v. 28). Vision and voice are together. Seeing and hearing are close one to the other. This is God's way of coming to this man, so that understanding the will of God for his life he can then engage in a ministry of understanding the needs of his people. The Seer is a man who sees what others do not see. He also hears what others do not hear. He is in a condition of mental and spiritual ecstacy in which God can cause him to respond to stimuli outside the ordinary channels of communication. Ezekiel was sensitive to the knowledge of God through the Holy Spirit and obedient to all that God demanded from him.

(4) *A pastor of knowledge.* After the vision came the voice. God's message to Ezekiel began, "Son of man, stand upon thy feet, and I will speak with thee" (2:1). This man was caught up under the spell of what had transpired

for he now knew something of the glory of God. It was imperative that the exiles should not lapse into the idolatry of their oppressors. A new generation was born in exile and was subject to the seductions and enticements of the new land and its ways. Ezekiel was young himself and knew the tragic possibilities of defection from the one, true and living God. In his pastoral spirit he was reinforced with divine knowledge so that he put himself in the same place as his people in their trial and temptation. He was the pastor alert and at attention in knowledge and thus ready for action. The divine energy was his for "the Spirit entered into me. . .and set me upon my feet." "A roll of a book. . .was spread before me. . ." (2:8-10). Here was the source of knowledge. He was told to "eat the roll and then go and speak to the house of Israel" (3:1-3).

(5) *A pastor of obedience.* God told Ezekiel to go and be with his people to share their lot. This he did. After vision came action; after listening came movement. He would not be guilty of the blood of his fellows in sinning against them by silence. He would speak to them the word of God, but not in absence. He says "I sat where they sat" (3:15). He was among his people by the river without saying anything for seven days. Just to be one of them was the best way to reveal his interest in them and his concern for their welfare. This is ever the principle of identification. The pastor cannot remain aloof or detached. He must be "one of them." The shepherd is always among his flock and the sheep hear his voice, but they are also conscious of his nearness at all times. So Ezekiel brought to Israel in captivity the knowledge that he was with them in their trial and affliction. He was sharing with them.

II. He Proclaimed the Divine Word to All, 2:1-5

The pastor's calling includes that of ministering the word of God to his people. Ezekiel was not found to fail at this point. He is known more for this than anything else. But it was not as a prophet alone that he served God--he ministered as a prophet with the pastor's heart. To speak the truth is to proclaim the whole counsel of God.

(1) *With conviction.* The words he spoke came from a heart aflame with the inspiration given by God for the task. He had heard the voice of God himself and this drove him to speak what the people needed to hear. He did not speak soft words or come to the people with blandishments and promises not of God. He did not have an easy assignment when God called him to his task. There would be those in exile who would argue that as they were now living in a foreign land they should make the best of it and engage in appeasement with their enemies. Perhaps they had so lost hope that they concluded they should become as their captors and compromise their religious faith for other heathen religions and ways. But Ezekiel soon told them—none of this! They were the elect people of God and chosen by God for a destiny yet to be fulfilled. As he *sat* where they sat he now *stood* before them to remind them of the divine will for them. He spoke with passion and conviction. He was a voice for God. He spoke as a faithful shepherd must speak—for the sake of the sheep and the lambs.

(2) *With authority.* The people recognized in his words the voice of God calling them back to renew their vows and keep the Covenant relation. Ezekiel told them how stupid and ignorant they were in disregarding the word of God. At least they knew that when he spoke no one else

would speak like that! Not that they responded at once
to his call or repented and turned away from their sins.
They still persisted in their rebellious spirit against God.
They became angry with their spiritual leader who spoke
with authority and were ready to let their wrath spill
over against him. Their ire was manifest to him, but a
shepherd who is not an hireling is not silenced either by
threats or bribes.

(3) *With watchfulness.* As Ezekiel reminded his people
of their sins and their neglect of God he also told them
the way back to the heart of God. Fearlessly he spoke to
them of needs to be met and deeds to be done. The truth
has a cutting edge not palatable to all. At the same time
he watched for their souls. He told them that "all souls
are mine, saith the Lord" (18:4). "The soul that sinneth
it shall die" (18:4). "I have set thee a watchman unto the
house of Israel; therefore hear the word at my mouth, and
give them warning from me" (33:7). Having delivered his
word of warning to Israel and telling of the coming
doom of her enemies, Ezekiel spoke again to his people.
Both the Northern Kingdom and the Southern Kingdom
had been taken into captivity. Jeremiah was with a remnant in Egypt. Ezekiel was with the captives in Babylon.
He still watched for his people and their salvation. Thus
in his fidelity to his calling he watches for their souls by
giving them the truth as received from God.

(4) *With mercy.* The end of exile was not to be total
annihilation but restoration. The judgments of God were
sure. The lamentations were wrung from bleeding hearts,
but the door of hope remained ajar. There was mercy
mixed with judgment. God had not forgotten his Covenant and there was a Remnant to survive. In the cure
of souls the shepherd will hurt his people by the truth he

proclaims, but at the same time he will bring to them the good-will of God for another day to dawn for them. He will teach and comfort. Naught for their comfort may be the major word, but mercy gleams intermittently in the many messages he brings to them. The New Covenant is promised for the new day for God's people. Here was the way out of their exile and the way of their renewal finally. Ezekiel saw the vision of dry bones in the valley (37) and predicted the restoration of the nation. Despondent though they might be, this was God's promise and pledge of the coming of the breath and wind of the Spirit. "Can these bones live?" The prophet's answer was one of assurance and faith "O Lord God, Thou knowest!" By the word of God in prophecy and the four winds of the Spirit, God's everlasting mercy was demonstrated once more.

III. He Conserved the Faith and Life of Many, 34:11-16, 31

The shepherd heart is from God who is the Shepherd, King, and Father of His people. Out of that comes the under-shepherd Ezekiel with his pastoral concern. The king of the nation was also characterized by these titles. What they failed to do in kingship for the nation God was doing on their behalf. Ezekiel foretold of a David or a Messiah who would be the fulfilment of this promise. Reading this we are turned at once to the New Testament picture of the Good Shepherd and the New Covenant. While Ezekiel manifested his compassion for the lost people the vision of Christ and the multitudes is greater.

Ezekiel tells of the Shepherd seeking or searching for the lost sheep of Israel—"For thus saith the Lord Jehovah: Behold, I myself, even I, will search for my sheep, and will seek them out. As a shepherd seeketh out his flock in the day that he is among his sheep that are scattered abroad, so will I seek out my sheep. . ." (vv. 11, 12). "And ye my sheep, the sheep of my pasture, are men, and I am your God, saith the Lord Jehovah" (v. 31). What a remarkable passage and distinctly it anticipates the New Testament idea of Christ the Good Shepherd and the pastors under him in the church as under-shepherds! As God the Lord was Israel's Shepherd, so Ezekiel was their under-shepherd. He had his work to do and was willing to serve them.

Sheep are easily led astray. The shepherd must guide them in safe ways and find pasturage for them. At night he protects them in the sheepfold. He is the door as he lies across the threshold or entrance. Robbers and wild beasts cannot prey upon the sheep when he protects them in this manner. The shepherd is ready to lay down his life for his sheep. He must maintain their strength and health in giving them the right food and refreshment. A faithful pastor does this as he watches over his flock. Ezekiel did this in exile among his own people.

What about the lambs of the flock? They, too, must be attended to when brought into the world and cared for as they grow. Ezekiel had the task of teaching the young among the exiles. He would remind them of their history as a nation. He would tell them of the mighty deeds of God in the Exodus. The Passover—in which they participated—was brought to them as a memorial and spur to holy living. They were taught that they were the people of God, the chosen and elect people. Ezekiel sought to conserve the flock at all ages and stages of growth. He withstood those who would rob the nation of its best years. The enemies who enslaved them in captivity were known, but also the faint-hearted and those of his own people who would compromise were involved. False prophets raised their voices and the people wished them to speak smooth things but not necessarily the truth. Ezekiel took his stand against them, "Behold, I have made thy face strong against their faces, and thy forehead strong against their foreheads. As an adamant harder than flint have I made thy forehead: fear them not, neither be dismayed at their looks, though they be a rebellious house" (3:8, 9). Ezekiel did not choose the easy way.

In the cloudy and dark day (v. 12) Ezekiel did not flag nor fail in his pastoral work. He knew the sorrow and the heartaches of the people. He recognized the disappointments of the long years of exile. He sensed that hope was sometimes almost gone. By his work among the exiles he believed that God would bring them out in safety and return them to their land. There was a future and his counsel brought new spirit to those who were responsive. In the visions granted him he had the assurance of that final vocation of the chosen people as a nation under God and serving him again.

Ezekiel's fellow-prophet Jeremiah also spoke of the shepherd heart and task. "I will give you pastors (shepherds) after mine own heart, who shall feed you with knowledge and understanding" (Jer. 3:15). Graphically John Bunyan in his *Pilgrim's Progress* has caught this picture and describes what Ezekiel faced and knew. The Delectable Mountains rise out of the heart of Immanuel's Land. This fine range falls away on the one side toward the plain of Destruction, and on the other side to the Celestial City. It was on these mountains that two travelers found and met the shepherds. They speak of *Knowledge* with his insights and attainments for such a work of the shepherd.

There was *Experience* with kindly eye and hard-earned wisdom. *Watchful* is the third of the shepherds and Ezekiel made much of being a watchman. The fourth is *Sincere* who has that gravity and bearing of the man to be trusted. These four shepherds of John Bunyan's imagination and interpretation might well be the summing up of Ezekiel. He saw the sheep in danger of straying to the plain of Destruction and he sought to lead his flock up to the Celestial City. It is this last vision which he sees and proclaims in Chapters 47 and 48. The day would come when "everything shall live whithersoever the river cometh" (47:9) and "Jehovah is there" (48:35). At the climax of history is the eternal city and the temple. Exiles dreamed of it when separated from their holy city and temple. Now in prospect lay the eternal sanctuary, a city all temple, God present.

Ezekiel is one of the most mysterious, yet one of the most entrancing, of the Hebrew prophets. He lived and labored in the most difficult times—when his people were in exile. Alone and solitary he accepted the commission of God and single-handed he carried out his task. His messages were preserved and written down so that more than his own people would benefit from his teaching. His pastoral outreach lay far beyond his own. He reinterpreted the disasters and doubts of his nation into the hopes and promises of better things. His final satisfaction lay in the promise of God's grace, "I will sprinkle clean water upon you, and ye shall be clean; from all your filthiness, and from all your idols will I cleanse you. A new heart also will I give you, and a new spirit will I put within you; and I will take away the stony heart out of your flesh, and I will give you a heart of flesh" (36:25, 26).

12

Daniel,
Steadfast in Crises

Daniel was carried away into captivity before Ezekiel, during the reign of Jehoiakim. Nebuchadnezzar was king of Babylon when Daniel was but a youth and his entire life was lived in exile. Like Joseph, he was destined to occupy one of the highest positions in the land and at the same time give his unswerving devotion to the God of his fathers. After the United Kingdom was established under Saul, David, and Solomon the nation of the Hebrews was divided into North and South in a Divided Kingdom. The North comprised the ten tribes and was known as Israel. These tribes were taken into captivity by Shalmaneser into Assyria and never returned. The South comprised two tribes and was known as Judah. These tribes were carried away into exile by Nebuchadnezzar and ultimately large numbers of them returned. Thereafter came a period for the nation as a Dependency during which Daniel in exile survived and gave his message. *That message concerned the sovereignty of God in history.* Daniel the seer saw the onward march of successive empires in relation to the Hebrew people. He shows that events are in the hand of Almighty God. History and prophecy intertwine as he speaks of his times and the ages to follow. Daniel is unimpeachable in character.

I. His Purpose, Daniel 1—4

A young man with an indomitable spirit is found in these chapters.

(1) *He purposed in his heart* (1:8). The issues of life are found here. What a man is seen to be and known to be finds basis in the inner life. There decisions are made and resolutions formed. Choice is determinative for character. The occasion was simple and at first sight seemingly not very important—what was to be eaten. At the court of the king many young Hebrew men were given places as servants. To test their loyalty and dependability Daniel and his three companions were trained in the language and learning of the Babylonian civilization. For their special service, this test was devised, to eat as all others ate. The commander of Babylon who supervised them was afraid that in their self-denial they might appear under-nourished and therefore the king would be displeased. But Daniel requests the test be granted and the result we know. Conformity in food and other things would have been defiling to the Hebrew with his laws of holy living and hygiene. Daniel had made up his mind in advance not to be defiled, hence the resolve. As a result "God gave them knowledge and skill in all learning and wisdom: and Daniel had understanding in all visions and dreams" (v. 17).

(2) *He returned answer with counsel and prudence* (2:14). The circumstances wherein Daniel was able to bear witness before a heathen court were part of his ap-

pointed work. After several years of training and culture Daniel and his friends were now engaged in their courtly service. Word came that the king had had a dream and was disturbed. The wise men of Babylon were called to find out what the dream was and give its interpretation. But no one could do this. Then someone recalled the young man Daniel and how he had proved by his fidelity to God that God honored such a person with wisdom and knowledge. Such no doubt lay partly in the human education acquired, but it is suggested here that divine insight and wisdom were given. When the experts failed, God had Daniel at hand to act. The king was shrewd in asking the Babylonish wise men to give the dream first, knowing that if they could do that what they would say would not be fictitious. Here is where Daniel demonstrated that he had nothing in himself but that what he received was God-given. The colossal image was at the heart of the vision and dream. Its instability and final destruction would prepare for an eternal kingdom—one coming from God. Thus Daniel brought the knowledge of God's will to the king and his kingdom.

(3) *He had in him the spirit of the holy god* (4:8). The next stage of Daniel's life was associated with his three friends, Shadrach, Meshach, and Abed-nego (3). They, too, were tested and in their refusal to bow to the great idol, the image of the king, they were cast into the burning fiery furnace. They were martyrs or witnesses as they lived with Daniel (who also must have stood with them). "But if not. . ." (3:18) gives the heart of their faith in accepting the consequences of their stand. They, too, shared Daniel's purpose of heart. Then Daniel was called again by the king to interpret another dream—this time showing the great tree. When the king spoke of Daniel

having the "spirit" this is the way of God's sovereignty causing this man to proclaim the source of Daniel's strength and power. It was not from himself but it was divinely imparted. The king was to acknowledge that God's kingdom was an everlasting kingdom (4:3) and that Daniel was a servant of that eternal kingdom.

II. His Persistence, Daniel 5

How strong is the spirit of Daniel in crises.

(1) *The crisis-hour* (vv. 1-5). When the heathen king, Belshazzar the son of Nebuchadnezzar, desecrated the vessels of the Temple he instigated his own downfall. How often in history have men been brought to ruin through indulgence in strong drink, for liquor is no respector of persons. Men in high places of privilege and responsibility are exposed to temptations thrice-heated. Prosperity and power can lead to corruption. Archaeology pays tribute to this occasion as historical truth. As the king did his sorry act the seven-branched candlestick cast its light upon the wall of the banquet room. This was the screen on which God was to write his message of judgment. The king saw the hand that wrote and conscience filled his heart with foreboding of doom. Revelry by night was the prelude to a crisis of judgment in the morning. Daniel's character was then revealed. Earlier he had shown his strength of faith in God and now in this dark hour he is ready to speak and stand for the truth.

(2) *The crucial test* (vv. 6-18). Nothing intimidated Daniel. He had no difficulty in deciphering the message on the wall. The king was "weighed and found wanting." Daniel was "that Daniel. . .whom my father brought out of Jewry. . ." (v. 13). In the hour of debauchery there

were those who remembered his name and that in him was "an excellent spirit" (v. 12). His influence was undimmed and his life untarnished. Daniel could remind this king of his father and how God bent him to his will. No bribe touches Daniel. No intimidation frightens him. He brought the message of judgment and doom to the king and the nation—for the enemy were soon at the gates —and he alone could interpret the mystic writing. "The God in whose hand thy breath is, and whose are all thy ways, hast thou not glorified" (v. 23). In this lies the sin of the king unmasked. The obscenity, the profanity of the king's behavior did not alter the divine sovereignty for his life—and rebellion brought ruin.

(3) *The coming honor* (vv. 19-28). Daniel had the distinction of standing unflinchingly. No reward of the State, however magnificent, could match the wonder of his faith and devotion. That was reward enough and in itself to please God and not man. Daniel was not like those who only do right if it is convenient or if it pays off. His acts were based on principle and not policy. Judgment came soon to the king and Daniel lived on to exercise greater influence in the nation. He never wavered but was faithful to the end. As the third ruler in the land he received acclamation and honor from the people. Like Joseph in Egypt he knew the privilege of power but he did not abuse that honor. All he had received he recognized was God's doing. He was but a steward of that providence and will.

III. His Praying, Daniel 6

The life of Daniel had no respite from tests and trials. His enemies sought out opportunities to trap him.

(1) *They sought to find occasion against Daniel* (v. 4).

In this situation we can easily see how Daniel was in danger. His enemies knew that he never deviated from his religious customs. All others in the nation had found it good policy to obey the wish of the king and the religious laws of idolatry and State worship. Daniel and his Hebrew companions were the exception. Yet Daniel had been elevated to the high office indicated already. Envy and jealousy played their part as others p'otted with devious ways to trap him and bring him into disrepute and ruin. They knew they could not turn him into an idolater but they schemed to have him neglect what he practiced.

(2) *His windows were open in his chamber toward Jerusalem* (v. 10). In this word lay the crucial test in the crisis now upon Daniel. Could his enemies make him defect from his regular practice? Was it possible to weaken the forces which were the strength of his life and character? Daniel could have continued his worship in prayer alone and out of sight and no one would have done much. But here on the roof-top and in sight of all, his chamber windows were open—the sign that he looked toward the Holy City and prayed to God. The steady habit of his life was not changed because of the threat from the evil forces arraigned against him. Circumstances could not alter his convictions. Perhaps spies reported what went on.

(3) *My God hath shut the lions' mouths* (v. 22). The jaws of the trap closed in on Daniel who refused to become an idol worshipper. The penalty was to be thrown into a den of lions. The new king Darius had faith that Daniel's God would be with him. The thrilling story carries its own message for all. No hurt was done to the prophet because he trusted in his God (v. 23). The

boomerang of judgment came back upon the evil plotters
and they suffered what they plotted for Daniel. Daniel's
God was praised and honored by the king for the whole
nation to know and copy. "So this Daniel prospered in
the reign of Darius and in the reign of Cyrus" (v. 28).
This is the reward for a man praying. Prayer is the
mighty force used by God for the upbuilding of character
and for the pulling down of the strongholds of evil. A
man in prayer to God is greater in influence than all
the armies of men.

IV. His Prophecying, Daniel 7—11

In this area of reporting there are those who question
any such idea that the future could be seen and that all
the prophet did was to forecast something pending on the
basis of shrewd judgment in the light of the trends. However, the Old Testament claims that part of its literature
is prophecy—not merely preaching to the immediate needs
of the people, but also looking into the future and, by
divine inspiration, foretelling. Examples are found in this
book of Daniel where the prophet speaks and out of
promise comes fulfillment. Certain of the visions recorded
find an out-working almost immediately.

(1) *The visions of Babylon.* Nebuchadnezzar had the
vision of the colossal man, an image with varying metals.
The interpretation was given by Daniel as that of a foreshadowing of world empires in succession. The Babylonian
empire was represented by the head of gold and Nebuchadnezzar was the head of his kingdom. The breast and
arms of silver introduce the Medo-Persian kingdom. The
brass of the belly and thigh tells of the Grecian empire.
Then comes the legs of iron, and the feet part of iron and
clay point to the Roman Empire yet to come. Finally,

there fell a stone which broke the image to pieces, after which the Stone became a great mountain and filled the earth. This Stone is declared to be a kingdom which God will set up, and which will stand forever; and just as Nebuchadnezzar stood for the kingdom of which he was the head, so this Stone is Christ. His kingdom is from above and is eternal and, therefore, indestructable.

After this Daniel himself was given a dream and visions as recorded in Chapter 7. Four winds of heaven strove upon the great sea. Out of that came four great beasts, different in kind one from the other. The first was like a lion, the second like a bear, the third like a leopard, and the fourth like something which was unknown before and whose likeness could not be given. "These great beasts, which are four, are four kings, that shall arise out of the earth" (v. 17) does not indicate their names, but we can compare these with the four metals of the colossal image of the man and find their similarity in structure and relationship. Obviously, this dream of Daniel's is a confirmation of what was earlier. History records the succession of Nebuchadnezzar, Cyrus, Alexander, and then the Roman Empire with many leaders. The "great seas" speaks of that background out of which came these empires and tells of the nations of the world at that time. Here are supremacy and might; strength and ruthlessness; speed and cruelty; with the fourth suggesting something terrible and dreadful in power and might.

(2) *The boundaries of revelation.* Close to the idea of prophecy lies the fact that God here unveils the future. The text clearly teaches that this is not something Daniel invented or surmised because he was a clear thinker and could read the signs of the times. There was no guesswork. Daniel as prophet is open in mind (as Peter was in

Matt. 16 when he was given the revelation of what he
said—Jesus is the Christ, the Son of God—*given by God*).
He is a channel for divine inspiration and thought finding expression in these pictures of the succession of world-
empires rising and falling. There was also the vision of
the Two Beasts (chap. 8) which is an intensification from
the previous vision of the Four Beasts. Then the Unveil-
ing of the Seventy Sevens or the years determined by God
(chap. 9) for events to come tied in with Jeremiah's
prophecy (Dan. 9:2 and Jer. 25:11, 12; 29:10). This told
that seventy years would be the limit of judgment and
exile for that time. Thus a period of 490 years was determined by God. Sixty-nine weeks of years—483 years commenced with the decree of Cyrus, and ended with the
Baptism of Jesus. Then the seventieth week commenced
and in the midst of it, the Messiah Jesus Christ was cut
off (9:24-27). (The destruction of Jerusalem with its
Temple in A.D. 70 marked the climax.)?

V. His Promotion, Daniel 12

After all the visions are recorded and Daniel's writing
is completed the summing up of his life and ministry is
given. Passing by the details of Chapter 11 the Scripture
of truth lies open. He sees the consummation of the ages
in relation to his own people the Jews. There is predicted
a time of trouble far worse than any have ever known
before. Beyond that is the bright hope of good over evil
and righteousness finally victorious. God allows much to
take place as the nations seek their own will, but he will
finally reveal himself as sovereign over all things. This is
the final word. Daniel speaks "I will show you the truth"
(11:1) and "what shall be the issue [or latter end] of these
things?" (12:8). Daniel stands between what has been

revealed to him and is now knowledge, and that which has not been revealed and is therefore unknown. When God unveiled what is found in the first part of the book Daniel could accept for the present. The future still had its secrets from him and there were areas of knowledge withheld from him.

Any scrutiny of Daniel's life will find that God honored this young man for several reasons.

(1) *His non-conformity.* In an age when it was popular to do what everyone else did and what would please the right people, Daniel dared to stand alone or with his three companions for the right and the truth. His Hebrew religion and his personal faith in God were never compromised. Neither bribery nor intimidation could influence him. No threats of persecution or suffering swayed him. He was no coward and his courage stands out in glorious deeds and words. All the misfortunes of being an exile in a strange land did not shake his spirit. In crises many he never wavered.

(2) *His prayerfulness.* The time when he dared to keep up the habit of daily devotions and worship before God is well known. There he refused to defect from his high standard of honor. In addition to that he also prayed for his country in intercession (cf. 9:1-19). There is the record of a remarkable prayer in which he identifies himself with his people in their sins and in their guilt. He prays in confession and pleads in intercession for his nation. His praying was based upon his study of the word of God (Jer. cf. Dan. 9:2). Knowledge and spiritual ardor were joined together.

(3) *His steadfastness.* The many tests and trials brought him ever into danger and possible death. The years were years of tension and frustration for his people. Yet he

went through many crises without deviating from his position of rectitude. He was not defiled by the indulgences of that era. He refused to be honored save by God's promotion and advancement. He, too, was weighed in the balances, and found *not* wanting! Upright in character and undismayed by the world around, he abides as one of God's noblemen.

13

Nehemiah,
Patriot in Action

After the captivities of Israel and Judah the exiles had
no opportunity to return until Cyrus arose to dispossess
the Babylonians of their empire. In the providence of God
a new beginning was made in the history of the chosen
people. Then remnants were recalled out of captivity and
finally returned to their own land. These events serve to
reveal the sovereignty of God in the movements of the
nation. Once united, then divided, later in captivity, they
ended in dependency. Back in their own land they were
not entirely free, but subject to the government of their
over-lord and ruler who placed them there. Through
these remnants God kept alive the hope of a coming
Messiah, the consciousness of national destiny, and the
knowledge of a mission to the world. Ezra first of all
pioneers in the effort of reconstruction followed by
Nehemiah whose life we unfold. Zerubbabel was another
vitally involved then. Their relationship is important.
Zerubbabel's work was the rebuilding of the Temple;
Ezra's the restoration of worship; and Nehemiah's, the

reconstruction of the city of Jerusalem. For awhile the work went on when Judah returned from exile, but slackness and loss of faith overtook them until Nehemiah arose to intervene to save his people. This involved him in the journey to Jerusalem and the permission of Cyrus had to be obtained first. We see what kind of man he was as a patriot and lover of his nation.

I. A Man of Patriotism, 1:1-3

An interval of twelve years lay between the work of Ezra and the coming of Nehemiah to Jerusalem. Nehemiah was the man who particularly engaged in the task of rebuilding the city walls. He continued the work begun under Zerubbabel. We have here something of *autobiography*. He tells his own story and gives a vivid, first-hand account of the ups and downs of his life and work in relation to his patriotic deeds. Neither the Greeks nor the Romans looked at the deeds of history in the way of the Hebrews. The latter looked at events in a religious vein and related everything to God. Thus religion is never a special sphere of human activity, but a synthesis of all. Nehemiah in acting as he did was motivated by religious concern.

God used Cyrus, king of Persia, to initiate much of what transpired on behalf of the Jews. "Jehovah stirred up the spirit of Cyrus" (Ezra 1:1). His proclamation and decree opened the door for a new beginning. Nehemiah at that time in the course of his ordinary duties and work is another instrument of God for the divine purpose. "The words of Nehemiah" are actually "the *history* of Nehemiah" (v. 1). A report had come from Palestine about its condition and now Nehemiah says, "I asked them concerning the Jews" (v. 2). In reporting this he speaks with vigor and concern, and there is a vitality which reveals the true heart of a man who loves his nation and his people. Patriotism is one of the ways in which God can use a man. In our day of world ideas of one world and united nations organizations, we need not despise or forget true patriotism. This God-given instinct has in it the highest and noblest ideals for service toward our native land and people. By means of it the heart is stirred and the life geared to action.

II. A Man of Commonsense, 1:4—2:8

The news about the "remnant" (v. 3) was the chief fact which dominated the mind of Nehemiah. He knew the messenger as "one of my brethren" (v. 2) and this was the background of the practical concern he showed.

(1) *The challenge of the work.* There in Jerusalem lay the task to be done. No one else had been able to complete it. He accepted this challenge. He recognized the ruined state of the Holy City, the place he loved. There was the religious center as well as the political center of his nation. He belonged there! When he heard of the Jews who were in great affliction and reproach, he visualized and sensed their predicament. They were poor and needy; they had little resources and no encouragement to labor. They were dispirited and had lost hope. With broken walls they were a prey to enemies and robbers as well as wild beasts. Ruins may be of interest to tourists who now visit ancient sites but in that time of Nehemiah the ruins spoke only of one thing—disaster and hopelessness! Thus he was challenged to do something.

(2) *The call to the work.* Brooding over the report received, he cried and mourned certain days (v. 4). Out of this came prayer and fasting (v. 5) in which he besought

God (vv. 6-11) on behalf of his people. The prayer is note-worthy in that he confesses the sins and shortcomings of his nation. He realizes how they have failed again and again. The corruption of unbelief and the baseness of breaking the commandments are there. He recognized that God was just in allowing them to spend years in captivity when they had slighted his love and mercy. Yet at the same time he also spoke to God about their Covenant relation as the elect people and their destiny as an instrument of God. God's promise to regather them was cited and pleaded as the basis for help now in the emergency. He spoke as one who was ready and willing to do anything for the Lord and prayed definitely for one thing —that he might have favor in the sight of king Cyrus before whom he stood at the post of duty.

(3) *The providence of God* (2:1-8) Nehemiah was the king's cupbearer. He had his duties to carry out and he could not relax. Only his spirit and his praying caused the king to see he was a man carrying something on his mind, a burden which was expressed in his sad face. The king was discerning and fair in judgment so that he sensed the sorrow of heart of Nehemiah (v. 2). Nehemiah was ready to give up the splendor of the court for the rigors of a neglected and blighted area of need. He asked God in prayer for help and now was the opportunity opened by God to ask the king for help. But even as he asked the king and told his story to him he also prayed in an ejaculatory spirit. "The king said, for what dost thou make request? *So I prayed to the God of heaven*" (v. 4). This is the practical aspect of the spiritual life. The vertical and the horizontal are together. God and man are joined in this experience. Ask man for help but pray

to God first. Thus through prayer, the mighty means of usefulness to the man of faith, the patriot acts.

III. A Man of Strength, 2:9-20

We have seen how practical Nehemiah was in his praying and asking. His boldness in asking the king for permission to do something is marked. He received strength from God and the imparted power was evident in a number of ways.

(1) *Courage in the face of criticism.* Of course there would be those who would not like his action. He had received "letters" (v. 7) from Cyrus giving him the right to proceed to Jerusalem and engage in his task. He needed supplies for rebuilding and these had to be obtained from certain sources (v. 8). He also required safe conduct which was granted (v. 7). All these details were covered well, but Nehemiah knew he would not receive the full support of all. Not even from those who lived within the ruins of Jerusalem. Sanballet (v. 10) was one who was "grieved" and disturbed that he had come to attempt what seemed an impossible task. Later, Sanballet and his cronies Tobiah and Geshem heard what was to be attempted, and they "laughed us to scorn" and imputed false motives of rebellion and implied that Nehemiah was not the kind of man for the position (v. 19).

(2) *Faith in the face of disaster.* The ruins were there and the unfinished work stared them in the face. Nehemiah and his few friends with him realistically assessed the situation. During the night he inspected the conditions first hand. Going around the ruined walls he saw what was involved was a herculean task. Alone at first, he gathered the information he needed before he invited others to join him. This was faith. Having prayed to God,

God would have him act in this way to implement his prayer. The co-operation of God's servant was given gladly and willingly in doing God's will.

(3) *Enthusiasm in the face of despair.* The strength or power displayed by Nehemiah was God-given. Considering the hopeless situation, it was remarkable and miraculous how this one man undertook to do this thing. Threats of intimidation, and disinterest on the part of most, might have deterred the stoutest heart. But Nehemiah was a man in whom the Spirit dwelled. The inspiration to build, the renewed interest of the people, and the consciousness of divine help enabled him to proceed in confidence that success would finally come. He did not minimize "the evil case, how Jerusalem lies waste" (v. 17). He did, however, urge and demand that the people "rise and build" (vv. 17, 18). The result of his spirit was contagious and "so they strengthened their hands for the good work" (v. 19). Nehemiah further testified against his enemies, "The God of heaven, he will prosper us" (v. 20). It was this spirit in him which routed his critics and shamed the half-hearted, so that finally the people as a whole responded to his call to build with him. In all this he is revealed as a strong man, inspired by God.

IV. A Man of Leadership, 3:1—4:6

This section of Nehemiah's memoirs is not dry and uninteresting, even though it relates names and statistics. The work was not carried out single-handed. We have here the roster or honor roll of those who took part in the enterprise. The skill and insight, the planning and leadership of Nehemiah are all seen in this way.

(1) *Who should work?* Obviously he sought for all the

people to share in this. There were those who refused, but across the remnant in Jerusalem he found people of all classes and conditions. One thing was necessary—they had to be people with minds open to the voice of God; they were people who knew they were of the Covenant, not aliens. They were priests, Levites, governors and nobles, young people, business men, and the common rank and file of the population. Reading their names is an education in itself for here the whole remnant people is found. Each group was united with the other in method.

(2) *Where should they work?* Nehemiah planned for them to toil where the need was greatest and also where there was any personal interest. They began at the center of the wall and then worked out in orderly fashion. System controlled their ways. The center was at the Temple and in the plan of Nehemiah everything was done so that each person had a share. There was unity in diversity of operations. Each one worked "next to" or "after" someone. The various gates are listed and many details given in this chapter so that we catch a glimpse of a vast operation following a definite plan and program. Here was the genius of Nehemiah's leadership.

(3) *How should they work?* The spirit of any work determines whether it will be completed or not. Example is given of the Tekoite nobles who "put not their necks to the work of the Lord" (v. 5). The Tekoite people worked but not their leaders. They were shirkers. In contrast was the way in which some others toiled—Ezer who was a "help," "another portion" (v. 19), and Baruch who worked "earnestly" (v. 20). Energy and zeal were found in many of Nehemiah's friends who followed his example and spirit. As the work proceeded Nehemiah

knew that there would be danger and opposition. Sanballet and his friends came again to intimidate and
threaten the workers (4:1-3). They sneered at and derided
the workers imputing the worst defeat of their efforts as
all in vain. However, Nehemiah once more rallied his
people with encouraging words as he prayed to God and
kept on building. "We built the wall. . .for the people had
a mind to work" (v. 6). Nehemiah's leadership was never
in doubt as the people had caught something of his spirit
which came from God.

V. A Man of Dedication, 4:7-23

When the wall was at half its height a new crisis came
in the derision of their enemies and a conspiracy to halt
any further building. Here Nehemiah shows himself to
be a man who refused to give up and who kept right on
in devotion to his task. Several elements are implied in
this.

(1) *Separation from hindrances.* This was a very valuable experience for all who shared with Nehemiah. The
enemies who sought to stop the work from going on,
used criticism at first and then increased their ridicule
and active assault. Some people cannot take the sneer and
the laugh against them. Nehemiah stood out against all
such. But violence by fighting was another matter now.
Nehemiah was ready for that also. Those who came to
interrupt the work by arms would find that he was pre-
pared for that—"we made our prayer to God, and set a
watch against them night and day" (v. 9). Prayer is God's
weapon to give strength and moral courage as well as
bring divine intervention when needed, but watching is
co-operating with God in what man can do in the fight.
Here is neither foolish independence of God, nor neglect

of human responsibility. They next cleared away the rubbish around the walls so that nothing would hinder them in their defense of the city. They became a separated people in clearing the issues and abandoning themselves to God under this plan.

(2) *Devotion to God's work.* A new spirit arose as they followed Nehemiah's dedication. He instilled in them the spirit of faith and courage, "Be not ye afraid of them: remember the Lord, who is great and terrible, and fight for your brethren, your sons, and your daughters, your wives, and your houses" (v. 14). He had appealed to them on the highest plane—the spiritual. God first was to be remembered. The fear of man passes when we are imbued with the faithfulness of God. He has given his promise and we are his people, therefore we can rely upon him in this day of battle, so ran the reasoning. The new spirit so inspired them that they planned to have half work with the trowels and the other half watch and defend with their swords and arms. They carried this out intently and devotedly. Such concentration paid off in renewed zeal and devotion. There was so much being done and so great a spirit that many of them found no time even to take off their clothes! "So we labored in the work" (v. 21) tells of the dedication of the people under Nehemiah. It was his spirit of consecration which imbued them with the zeal to carry on at the crucial hour of danger.

VI. A Man of Judgment, 5—13
In his remaining memoirs Nehemiah gives us several glimpses of his character and the influence of his work. Success came at last to his efforts and the wall was finished. His judgment and discernment were acute and

far-seeing. He had planned well and he carried through his plan to the end.

(1) *Magnanimity*. His greatness of soul and unselfishness is noteworthy. His choice was ever impartial in disputes and his own conduct was ever above reproach. As time went on new problems arose. Some of the people exploited their poorer brethren. "I consulted with myself, and contended with the nobles" (5:7) is a revelation of this man's excellent spirit. As a judge he did wisely and well in settling cases. He even surrendered his own private rights for the public good. That was a direct contribution to right wrongs and keep his record true—"so did not I because of the fear of God" (5:15).

(2) *Discernment*. His wise judgments and words are unforgettable in this record. A new day of reconstruction for a waste city brings other problems of human relations, in civic and social ways. The man who built now was rebuilding a new order. "So the wall was finished" (6:15) crowned his life work but brought him new responsibilities. He was imperiled by enemies; intimidated by schemers; and insulted by those who hated him. He discerned what took place and was able to stand in that testing time. No work of God ever takes place without opposition. Nehemiah was able to complete the task unscathed because of the quality of his character.

(3) *Humility*. This was the crowning mark of his spirit. He sought nothing for himself. Success was God's. Benefits were for the people. The work was completed as ordained. He spoke not much of himself. He was modest in act. He gave God the glory in everything. Later, the secret was made known, "the joy of the Lord is your strength" (8:10). That was his secret as the patriot. "I

came to Jerusalem, and understood" (13:7). In after years, still the same man who knew the ways of God for his people and his place in service.